Alison Lloyd is old enough to have written 10 books, including Do You Dare: *Bushranger's Boys*, Our Australian Girl: *The Letty Stories*, *Year of the Tiger* and its sequel *Battle of the Jade Horse*.

Terry Denton has written or illustrated a vast number of amazing books, including the world-famous Treehouse series (with Andy Griffiths) and the picture books *Jandamarra* and *Boomerang and Bat* (with Mark Greenwood).

Neither of them are nearly old enough to have lived through any of the events in this book, but they both did a LOT of research. They have worked together on two books about China's history: the CBCA-shortlisted *Wicked Warriors and Evil Emperors* and *Dragons, Devils and Rebels*. They both live in Melbourne – the right way up at least some of the time.

THE UPSIDE-DOWN HISTORY OF DOWN UNDER

Alison Lloyd

Terry Denton

PUFFIN BOOKS

PUFFIN BOOKS

UK | USA | Canada | Ireland | Australia
India | New Zealand | South Africa | China

Penguin Books is part of the Penguin Random House group of companies
whose addresses can be found at global.penguinrandomhouse.com.

Penguin
Random House
Australia

First published by Penguin Random House Australia Pty Ltd, 2018

1 3 5 7 9 10 8 6 4 2

Text copyright © Alison Lloyd, 2018
Cover and internal illustrations © Terry Denton, 2018

The moral rights of the author and illustrator has been asserted.

Cover and text design by Bruno Herfst © Penguin Random House Australia Pty Ltd
Colour separation by Splitting Image Colour Studio, Clayton, Victoria
Printed in China

 A catalogue record for this
book is available from the
National Library of Australia

978 0 14 378866 9 (hardback)

penguin.com.au

P29 Image used with kind permission of Murujuga Land and Sea Council; P57 McRae, Tommy.
National Library of Australia, nla.obj-153003344; P88 Allen, George S & Stockdale, John. National
Library of Australia, nla.obj-230626173; P132 National Library of Australia nla.obj-135226428;
P152 Flogging a convict at Moreton Bay, 1836, from *The Fell Tyrant or The Suffering Convict* by
William Ross, London, 1836, 365/R, State Library of New South Wales; P178 Governor Arthur's
Proclamation to the Aborigines, ca. 1828-1830, Mitchell Library, State Library of New South Wales;
P196 Calvert, Samuel (artist.) 1865, State Library of Victoria; P205 State Library of Victoria, Image
PN05/05/77/00; P228 National Library of Australia; P251 'Resuscitation set, 1801-1850', Science
Museum, London. CC BY; P261 Ducote, Alfred & McLean, Thomas. National Library of Australia
nla.obj-135585009; P291 Federation Celebrations 11 May 1901, Museums Victoria Collections,
https://collections.museumvictoria.com.au/items/2005624.

This book acknowledges the traditional custodians of the land down-under and pays respects to elders past and present.

Thank you to those whose stories have been included. Not every story in our diverse history can be told here. But may this upside-down history put a few things back the right way up.

———————→

CONTENTS

CONTENTS

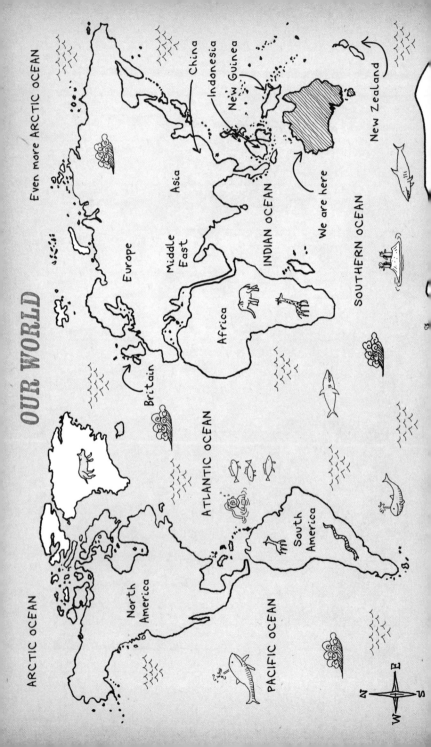

flies
seagull
chip

INTRODUCTION

If you ever wondered how we got to be Australia . . .

This is the book for you.

If you ever wanted to go back to the dinosaurs or the Dreaming . . .

This is the book for you.

If you've heard about convicts, captains or colonies – but you don't know how they fit together . . . If you love to read about rebels, riches, rights and wrongs, or adventures across the seas . . . If you like truth that's stranger than fiction . . .

This is the book for you.

This book puts all that and more together, in ways you might not expect. It might even turn some of your ideas upside-down.

For example, an Englishman called Captain James Cook was definitely not the first person to discover the land down-under. The story of our country started thousands and thousands of years before him.

To some of the people who came here later, this land seemed upside-down and back-to-front. But for others it was the right-way up and right-way round all along.

The same goes for this history. This book goes up to 1901, when we became a nation, not today. And some of that history looks wrong-way round to us now. Some parts are mean, tough or crazy. But some of it is epic, brave or smart. Some of it is yet to be told. But all of it is ours.

To explore the ups and downs, ins and outs of Australia's story, read on!

Aboriginal and Torres Strait Islander readers are warned that this book contains names and stories of people who have died.

Note on the sources used in this book: (Not the sauces you put on a sausage.) There is evidence for all the history in this book. Rocks and fossils have been studied by scientists. People also left objects behind that have been found by archaeologists. Other people wrote down their experiences in letters, journals, newspapers and books. And in some cases there is spoken history too, passed down the generations. Some quotes have been edited to make them easier to read. If you want to know where any of the information came from, and learn much, much more about our history, visit alisonlloyd.com.au

Note on the notes: If a word is complex you might find a note on the pronunciation or meaning in the margins of the page.

LAND ON THE LOOSE

The upside-down story of Down Under starts with a piece of land that went for a swim. This piece had been joined up with the rest of the world in one giant landmass called Pangaea. But 200 million years ago a part got loose. It broke off and took itself away. We now call that continent 'Gondwana'. At the time it was not known as anything, since nothing there could talk. Humans didn't come into the picture until a lot later.

It didn't float exactly, more like rumbled and shifted. Very, very slowly. It moved south at just a few centimetres a year. The big chunk of land broke up as it moved and came to rest on the other side of the world. Then it had a long holiday down near the South Pole.

Continent: a very large area of land with ocean around it.

'PANGAEA', THE SUPERCONTINENT
THE WORLD ABOUT 250 MILLION YEARS AGO

Before the big break-up, the world's continents were clumped together in a supergroup.

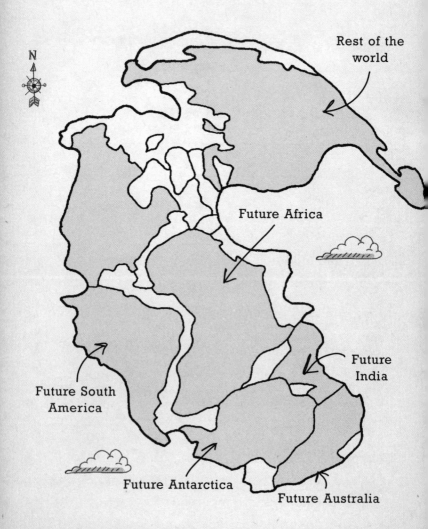

Rest of the world

Future Africa

Future India

Future South America

Future Antarctica

Future Australia

WHAT A DIFFERENCE 125 MILLION YEARS MAKES
THE WORLD IN THE CRETACEOUS PERIOD
(ABOUT 125 MILLION YEARS AGO)

By this stage, the supergroup was splitting up. The pieces were drifting apart, and the map started to look like a broken-up jigsaw.

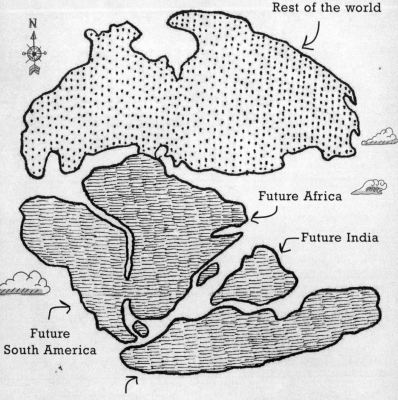

Rest of the world

N

Future Africa

Future India

Future South America

Future Antarctica, Australia, New Zealand and New Guinea, still heading south

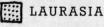 LAURASIA

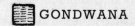 GONDWANA

Cretaceous: said 'cret-ay-shus'. The time period from 145–66 million years ago. You might have noticed that the dates for this part of our upside-down history get lower as the world gets older. Don't worry – they start going up again soon!

5

CRETACEOUS PARK

Gondwana was anything but empty. Even though it was near the South Pole, Gondwana didn't have any ice caps. It was not so freezing there then, although it was very dark in winter – there was no sunshine for up to four months a year.

Gondwana was like a zoo of amazing animals and plants. It was covered in forests of pine trees, ferns and moss. It wasn't quite like Jurassic Park, because the Jurassic period was just about over when Gondwana went south. There were no tyrannosaurus or triceratops here. But reptiles still ruled through the Cretaceous period. There were definitely dinosaurs down-under. And they were like nowhere else on earth.

DINOSAURS OF DISTINCTION

Australia had some truly outstanding beasts.

Ozraptor: the oldest dinosaur found in Australia.	3m long × 1m high, 100kg, lived about 170 million years ago, ate meat.
'Cooper', a titanosaur: the biggest dinosaur found in Australia, found so recently that it doesn't have a scientific name yet.	About 30m long, 30–40 tonnes, lived 95–98 million years ago, ate plants.
Qantassaurus: the only dinosaur named after an airline, but it couldn't fly and wasn't even a bird.	1.5m long × 0.7m high, 45kg, lived 110 million years ago, ate low-growing plants, like ferns.

Minmi: the toughest of the Australian dinosaurs, with armour even on its stomach. We know this because we have found about 90% of its bony bits.

3m long × 1m high, 100kg, lived 105 million years ago, ate seeds, fruit and ferns.

Leaellynasaura: the smallest Australian dinosaur. It was light and speedy, with big eyes for seeing in the dark polar winter. It might have had feathers.

1m long × 40cm high, the weight of a human toddler, lived 110 million years ago, ate plants.

Dromornis stirtoni: one of the world's largest birds, which also goes by the awe-inspiring name of Stirton's Thunderbird. It was flightless and lived in the north of Down Under.

3m high, up to 500kg, lived 8–6 million years ago, maybe ate meat, because they had a hooked beak.

Leaellynasaura: said 'lee-a-lin-a-sore-a'. Named after the daughter of the discoverer. **Dromornis stirtoni:** think of it as saying a 'drom-ornis' (running bird) that can 'stir Tony' and you'll say it right.

Unknown sauropod: the long-necked, four-legged owner of the world's biggest footprint, which was big enough to squash an adult human underneath.

Footprints are 1.7m wide, lived 130 million years ago, ate trees.

LIGHTNING *CLAW*

We only have one piece left of Australia's biggest known carnivore – just one long, curved claw.

About 110 million years ago, that claw belonged to a 7-metre monster, chasing its prey around the country. Now if you hold the fossil up to the light, it flashes, as if there are sparks of lightning inside. That's because the claw has turned into opal. It was found at Lightning Ridge in New South Wales (NSW), and that's how the place got its name.

It's funny that even though dinosaurs are Australia's oldest animals, scientists are still discovering new ones. One of the most recent finds was a set of sauropod footprints in 2016. So even as you read this, you might be sitting above the bones of some fantastic, undiscovered creature.

I lost a claw!

BIGGER ≠ BETTER

The later dinosaurs had to share Gondwana with much smaller creatures, like fish, cockroaches, fleas, crabs and water beetles.

They all got along together until about 85 million years ago. Then a section of land broke away from Gondwana and went to seek its fortune by itself. That bit would later be known as Aotearoa or New Zealand. The remaining parts of Gondwana went on as usual until around 65 million years ago, when there was a huge (and mysterious) change ...

Dinosaurs became extinct. Not just down-under, but all across the world. Nobody knows exactly why.

It was probably because a meteorite crashed into the earth near Mexico, blowing mountains of the earth's crust sky-high. Also, a volcano in India

Aotearoa: said 'Ow-tee-ah-raw-a'.

blew up. A real double whammy. The sky probably went black and rained burning shards of rock.

The disappearance of the dinosaurs doesn't seem to have bothered the other animals too much. They just took over the dinosaurs' place in the ecosystem. By 55 million years ago, the pieces of Gondwana were home to frogs, birds, bats, bandicoots and crocodiles.

ZOO *ON* THE MOVE

Another 10 million years after that, the zoo took off again. The land we now call Australia (plus the bit we call New Guinea and some other islands) waved goodbye to Antarctica and moved back north. Not exactly to where it is now, but fairly close.

Ecosystem: The way plants and animals and the environment fit together.

Australia is actually still on the move. You probably haven't noticed, because it's not in a hurry. If you are in school, then we've moved less than half a metre since you were born.

BIG BEASTIES

Nothing that looked like a human had disturbed the peace anywhere in the world yet, but some of the animals on this new continent would have looked familiar to you.

They were like modern Australian animals, but with a BIG difference – their size. We call them megafauna, which means 'super-sized animals'. Like dinosaurs, they often have super-sized names as well.

BIG SORT-OF-FRIENDLY GIANTS

Which one of these would you prefer to bump into in the dark? Or keep for a pet?

Zaglossus hacketti	A sheep-sized echidna, with a sticky tongue seven times as long as yours. It stood on its back legs and used its long nose and claws to get into termite mounds.

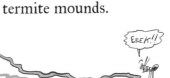

EEEK!!

Sthenurus	A 3m-long kangaroo that stood higher than a human and probably walked, not hopped.

Genyornis	A giant emu, 2m tall with massive legs.

There is no easy way to pronounce mouthfuls like **Zaglossus hacketti**, **Sthenurus** or **Genyornis** – try breaking them into bits (like 'za-gloss-us') and be glad it isn't *you* breaking them into bits.

| **Diprotodon** | The largest marsupial ever. A 2-tonne ball of fur that looked a bit like a bear and ate plants. It had a big head with a knobbly bony bit in the front, but most of its skull was empty space so it had a very small brain. |

| **Zygomaturus** | A marsupial with horns like a rhino. |

| **Simosthenurus** | A creature the same size and shape as a large kangaroo, except with a stubby snout like a koala and only one toe. It was heavy and probably slow, had very big noseholes, and might have been very loud (imagine herds of mooing roos). |

| **Anthropornis Nordenskjoeldi** | A penguin as tall as a person and a lot heavier. It wandered around Down Under 40 million years ago. |

Zygomaturus trilobus	A bull-sized marsupial with a large snout, and possibly tusks and claws for digging roots.

And those were just the plant eaters. There were also Gondwanans who could make you a goner.

IN THE LION'S DEN

In Western Australia (WA) there's a place called Tight Entrance Cave. The cave is near a river, so there would have been lots of juicy animals in the area. You can only get in and out by climbing through a hole in the roof.

Thousands of claw marks are still on the walls. Big ones and baby ones. Some of the claw marks are as high as 3 metres off the floor.

If you had been adventurous or silly enough to enter the cave 50,000 years ago, you would not have made it out.

It was a perfect den for a family of giant marsupial lions.

Thylacoleo carnifex

Its name means 'pouch lion flesh-eater'. It had 4- to 6cm-long teeth that fitted together like pairs of scissor blades on powerful jaws. It had very big front limbs with claws and opposable first toes so it could climb trees. It weighed about the same as a modern leopard and could have jumped on its prey from above. It probably dragged its dinner back up into the trees, like leopards still do, to keep it out of the reach of other creatures, such as…

Thylacoleo/thylacine: said 'thigh-la-col-ee-o' and 'thigh-la-seen'. The thylacoleo is the ancestor of the thylacine, which we will meet on the next page.

Quinkana fortiro-strum	A land crocodile that wasn't as heavy as a saltwater croc, but made up for that in speed with its hoof-like feet.
Propleopus oscillans	A giant rat-kangaroo as heavy as a small child. It had slicing  teeth with grooves, and probably ate small animals, insects, eggs and plants.
Megalania prisca	A gigantic 1-tonne goanna, with teeth serrated along one edge like a steak knife.
Wonambi naraco-ortensis	A 100kg, 6m-long python with a head the size and shape of a shovel, and hundreds of tiny teeth. It might have lurked beside water-holes or hid in rocky areas to ambush its prey.

GONE *THE* TIGERS

Thankfully you don't need to worry about lions on your way to school. But one prehistoric predator nearly made it to the modern day.

Tasmanian tigers, or thylacines, were striped animals that looked a bit like a dog or wolf. They had a tail like a kangaroo and carried up to four cubs in a pouch on their stomach.

Thylacines could open their jaws wider than a great white shark, to 120 degrees. That would have made going to the dentist easy, except that they didn't.

Thylacines first appeared around 30 million years ago. At least 10 species of them hunted in forests down-under. They disappeared from the mainland about 3300 years ago, probably because they didn't get on with dingoes, which arrived about 5000 years ago (the first animals introduced here by humans). But thylacines lived alongside Tasmania's original people for 35,000 years, until in less than 300 years Europeans hunted them to extinction.

WHAT'S NEW?

Not all prehistoric predators are extinct. Australia still has a deadly variety of large reptiles, including five large species of goanna, two sorts of crocodile and five large pythons.

We now have about 3300 species of animals that are found nowhere else, and that's not counting insects because there are so many of them buzzing around. Nine out of ten Australian plants, or 21,000 species, are unique.

Apart from its predators, Down Under was quite peaceful for millions of years. For a long, long time there were no humans around for the megafauna to munch on.

Over in Africa, fossils suggest that upright crea-tures emerged among the apes 3 million years ago. It wasn't until 100,000 years ago that scientists believe our ancestors – modern human beings – walked out of Africa. They were on their way to conquer the world.

Before they made it this far, though, a massive event would shake the region. And the effects would eventually reach our shores.

Species: said 'spee-sees', meaning a group of living things.

THE BIG BANG

In another broken-off bit of Gondwana, huge pressure was building beneath the surface. Boiling magma was rising to the earth's crust. Then, about 70,000 years ago, the lid blew off the surface and Mount Toba, in modern Indonesia, erupted.

Mount Toba was not a particularly big mountain. But when it blew, it was the biggest eruption the world had seen for 2 million years. It left a 100-kilometre-long hole, called a crater. That's a hole bigger than Sydney or Melbourne.

It burped out so much lava it could have covered the whole of Tasmania in rock 10 metres deep. Fortunately for the animals of Tasmania, the volcano was too far away to

Magma: sounds like a choc-coated icecream but is actually very melty rock and gas found inside the Earth.

actually do that. But it did blow an enormous cloud of ash across the area of the world that is now India and Africa.

HOW BIG *WAS THIS* BANG?

The biggest volcanic eruption in recorded history was Mount Krakatoa, an Indonesian island that blew up in 1883. That explosion destroyed most of the island and set off tsunamis that killed more than 36,000 people. How did Mount Toba compare?

Krakatoa	Toba
13,000 times as powerful as the Hiroshima atomic bomb.	130,000 times as powerful as the Hiroshima atomic bomb.
20 cubic kilometres of rock was blown into the air.	3000 cubic kilometres of rock was blown 40km into space. 50–400m of molten rock flooded hundreds of kilometres in every direction; Up to 5000 million tonnes of sulphur gas turned into clouds of sulphuric acid.

| Ash was carried 200km away. | India (2500km away) was covered in ash 3m deep. |

After the eruption, the sun would have been blacked out for weeks or months. Without sunlight, winter struck the world. Many plants and animals died. It would have been a terrifying time for people.

HUMAN FALLOUT

So when their homes became unsafe and food got hard to find, we can guess that people did what they still do – they ran for their lives.

Maybe the survivors in Asia got into boats. They might have sailed away looking for somewhere new to live. Perhaps this is when people first discovered the land down-under. Or perhaps they just moved closer.

We're not sure, but it seems that not too long after Mount Toba blew up, the land down-under was visited by its first humans.

And they were here to stay.

This is how we think people first spread across the world, based on ancient human remains found in different places. But scientists are still arguing exactly who moved where and when. (The 'k's on this map stand for thousands of years.)

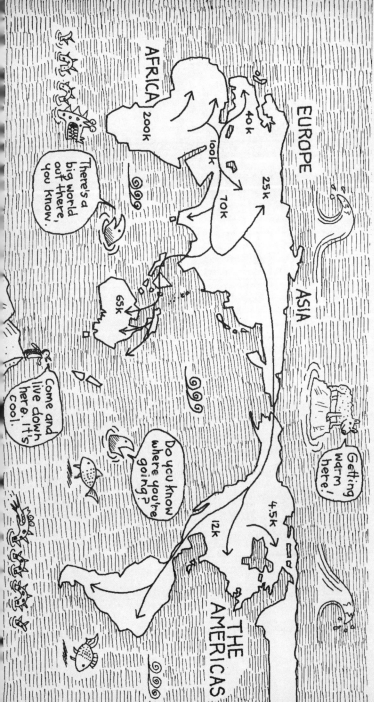

BOAT PEOPLE

We'll never know exactly when the first
Australians came, or how. Some Aboriginal
stories say that people came out of the land right
here. DNA scientists think they arrived in the
north of the continent (see the map on page 23).

Maybe one day a canoe full of adventurers
went out to sea from Indonesia. They saw
the smoke of far-off bushfires and paddled
towards it. Finally they pulled up on a beach,
ready to explore this new land. Maybe a group
of exhausted fishermen washed up on a raft.
They had drifted away from their fishing spot
and were hopelessly lost. Maybe the new
arrivals were refugee families, searching for
somewhere safe. Or maybe they were running
from the law.

NO **WAY** HOME

Whoever those people were, they probably set up
camp on the north coast. Or in what we now call
New Guinea, which was still joined to the continent.
They might have come in bark canoes like Aboriginal
people still used many thousands of years later. Bark
canoes can fit five or six people, and you can even
build a small clay fireplace in the middle.

But bark doesn't stand up to rough seas for long.
It's more likely that people came in bamboo rafts
or boats. Bamboo floats very well – it has its own
waterproof coating so it doesn't get soggy and sink.

There's a lot of bamboo growing in Asia, where
the people probably came from. But there was none
down-under. So once the people got here, there was
no way back.

STONES AND BONES

At this time, humans across the world were in what
we call the Paleolithic period or the Stone Age.
They weren't using metal, let alone pottery or paper
or plastic or phones, but they were creative.

When they got here they made tools out of rock,
used fire, painted art and carved jewellery.

Note: All speech balloons have been translated into Modern English for your convenience.

We mostly know how people lived then from buried evidence. Stones and bones have survived in caves for thousands of years.

ANCIENT RECORD HOLDERS

Archaeologists keep making new discoveries – so the original Australians are still breaking records today. They even have some impressive world firsts.

- The oldest human home in Australia is Madjedbebe rock shelter near Kakadu in the Nothern Territory (NT). It is 65,000 years old. The world's oldest ground-edge axe was found here too.
- The oldest human remains in Australia were found at Lake Mungo in NSW. 'Mungo Man' was about 50 years old when he was buried, but his bones have lasted another 43,000 years or so. The sand around his body was stained pink, which means that he was painted with red ochre.

Ochre: said 'oh-ker', meaning coloured earth or clay.

- 'Mungo Lady' had the world's oldest known cremation, 42,000 years ago. What that means is that her dead body was burnt. Then her bones were smashed and buried. Both burials show that all those tens of thousands of years ago people cared for each other even after death like we do now.
- Australia's oldest rubbish heaps also go back thousands of years. Shell middens are piles of shells left after families feasted on seafood. One midden in Queensland is as tall as a two-storey house, 13 metres high. It has about 9 billion shells. But it's only a thousand years old, just a baby compared to Madjedbebe's 25,000-year-old midden of seashells and animal bones.
- And Australia might have the oldest map in the world – a rock carving in the desert of WA that shows where to find water.

We just ate 9 billion oysters!

My tummy hurts!

THE DREAMING

With the arrival of humans, the land down-under got an extra dimension. The people felt an invisible connection between themselves, everything in their country and the spirit world. This connection is called different names in Aboriginal languages: *tjurkurrpa* and *altjeringa* are two of them. In English it's called the Dreaming.

In the Dreaming, spirit beings formed everything. They gave laws and country to the people. People came from the land and belonged to it. That connection never stopped. It's still real for Aboriginal people today.

> The land owns us. It grows all of us up. We're living with family: from this ground, up to all the trees around, to the clouds, birds, animals and reptiles.
>
> Tjilpi Bob Randall, Yankuntjatjara elder, Uluru

Murujuga National Park has tens of thousands of rock carvings, more than anywhere else on Earth. This image was carved into red rock when thylacines still roamed all across Down Under. If you missed the thylacines, flip back to page 18.

AN ANCIENT AUSTRALIAN ART GALLERY

The world's biggest outdoor gallery, with the world's oldest surviving portraits, is in WA. Some of the carved images may have been there for 25,000 years. It's as close as we can get to seeing pictures of the earliest Australians and their world.

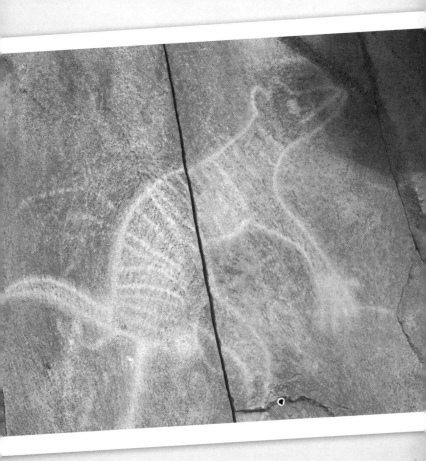

LONG MEMORIES

Although the first Australians didn't have books, they did tell stories. And the stories passed down from generation to generation still make sense.

In the Flinders Ranges in South Australia (SA), an Adnyamathanha man had been told about rock shelters by elders. The campsite he found turned out to be 50,000 years old.

In Queensland, the Gugu-Badhun people have a story of how fire once ran down the rivers, the air was full of dust and people died. Scientists recently worked out that the Kinrara volcano erupted there 7000 years ago. So the memories have survived for 230 generations.

THE LICE HEIST

The Dharawal people in NSW remember their history like this: Long ago all the animals lived in another land. One day they decided to look for better hunting grounds across the sea. The whale had a big bark canoe, but he wouldn't lend it to the others.

The starfish said to him, 'You have lots of lice on your head! Let me pick them out for you.'

The whale tied his canoe to a rock and put his

head in the starfish's lap. While the whale relaxed, the starfish gave a secret signal to the other animals. They sneaked down the beach and pushed off.

'Is my canoe all right?' the whale asked.

'Yes,' said the starfish, tapping a piece of bark by his foot. 'This is it right here.'

The starfish scratched the whale's head right next to his ears so he wouldn't hear the splash of the canoe's oars. But suddenly the whale spotted his canoe disappearing. He was furious. He beat the starfish up, which is how the starfish got its ragged look. The starfish also injured the whale, putting a hole on the top of his head.

The whale jumped into the water and chased the canoe for days and nights. And he still cruises along the coast, spouting water through the hole in his head. The other animals made it to a new land and became the first people of Australia.

THE STORY SO FAR...

230 million years ago
The first dinosaurs evolve from other reptiles

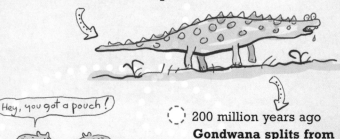

Hey, you got a pouch!

200 million years ago
Gondwana splits from Laurasia, breaking up the supercontinent

85 million years ago
Australia, New Guinea and Antarctica say farewell to New Zealand

65 million years ago
Dinosaurs go extinct Megafauna and mammals take the stage

40 million years ago
Australia and New Guinea wave goodbye to Antarctica

70,000 years ago
Mount Toba erupts

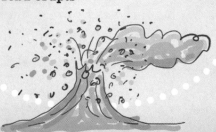

People arrive in northern Australia or New Guinea

At least 65,000 years ago People are living in Arnhem Land in NT in rock shelters

People start to move south

43,000 years ago Mungo man is buried in NSW

35,000 years ago People make it to Tasmania

28,000 years ago The oldest Australian rock art that still exists is painted

Don't stop now. There's much more to come . . .

Note on the dates: In prehistoric Australia, there were no calendars. That's why it's called 'pre-history'. These dates are best guesses by scientists today. For example, the more evidence we find, the longer it seems Aboriginal people have been here.

Possum skin coat

THE DEEP FREEZE

Bit by bit, the Earth began to turn cold. A new Ice Age had begun.

It reached its peak about 20,000 years ago. Life down-under became cold and miserable for everybody and everything. Worst of all was a terrible drought that came with the chill. We think of a drought as something that happens when it's hot, but this drought was caused by icy weather.

It was cold enough to freeze more of the sea, so the sea level dropped and less rain fell. This also meant less cloud, so the nights got colder. Many plants couldn't survive. Because there were fewer plants, the topsoil blew away in huge dust storms. Without food and shelter, many of the animals died too.

The snowline – where snow falls in winter – came a lot lower. People could only survive in small protected valleys. They lived in little groups, cut off from each other. Food was very hard to find.

It sounds bad but actually the people of Down Under were lucky. The continent had moved north at the perfect time. If it had still been in the Antarctic Circle, all life would have gone into permanent deep freeze.

The megafauna coped badly. Perhaps they had already come off worse in their battles with people. It's hard for large animals to find places to hide, especially if the weather is bad and hungry people are after you.

The people and the small animals managed to survive. But the megafauna didn't make it out of the Ice Age.

AUSTRALIA NOW

DOWN UNDER IN THE ICE AGE
AUSTRALASIA ABOUT 14 THOUSAND YEARS AGO

This is how our part of the world looked by the Ice
Age. It's much more like today than millions of years
ago if you compare it to the maps on pages 4–5. But
you can also see a lot more land around the edges
of Australia and its neighbours than we have today.
Mainland Australia and nearby islands, even Tasmania
and New Guinea, were all part of one big landmass.

THE DANGERS OF DEFROSTING

Around 15,000 years ago, the weather cheered up. The globe warmed. The sea thawed. It was too late for the megafauna. It was good news for everyone else, except for the floods.

Big chunks of land disappeared under water, including most of the land bridge to New Guinea. But about 7300 years ago, people made the best of the warm climate and moved onto some of the new islands off northern Australia in what we now call the Torres Strait.

It was especially tough for the people living furthest south. The path between Tasmania and the rest of Australia became a home for fishes.

Thousands of Tasmanian people were cut off from their mainland relatives. From then on, they were alone on their island. For company, they had Tassie tigers and Tassie devils, which soon became extinct on the mainland. But Aboriginal people were resilient. They were here to stay.

THE STORY HOTS UP...

20,000 years ago
The Ice Age is at its coldest

The megafauna are frozen

15,000 years ago
The weather slowly begins to improve

uh,oh!

I told you we should learn to fly.

24,000–14,000 years ago
Meanwhile in the rest of the world, people finally arrive in North America from Siberia

12,000 years ago
Melting ice caused by the warmer weather separates Tasmania from mainland Australia

8000 years ago
Melting ice floods the Torres Strait and separates Australia from New Guinea

7300 years ago
People come back to live in the new Torres Strait Islands

5000 years ago
Dingoes arrive in Australia

Hey, everybody! I'm here!

4500 years ago
Over in Africa, the first pyramid is built by Egyptians

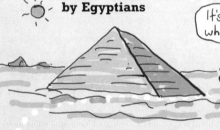

It's good, but where's the front door?

3300 years ago
Thylacines disappear from the mainland

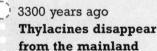

I'm off!

700 years ago
Hooray! People arrive in New Zealand

And the story continues . . .

HOW TO SURVIVE ON A DESERT ISLAND

Even in warm weather the land down-under wasn't always easy to get along with. People discovered that it also liked to turn on droughts, fires, floods and cyclones. Could people live with all of these ups and downs? The short answer is ... yes.

After the Ice Age, those first Australians spread out across the continent again. They didn't just cling to the coast where there was water and lots of animals and plants to eat. They made even the hottest, driest deserts their home.

How did they do it?

FOLLOWING *YOUR FOOD*

In some areas, the secret to survival was to travel light and keep on your toes. Each family group moved around on its own country, with a plan to follow the food.

If you were a Yawuru kid in WA, when the wind turned cold it was time to fish for salmon on the beach. For a Wik-Mungkan kid on Cape York in Queensland, while the grass was long your family fished and made bark food bowls. Then when the grass dried, you travelled inland to fill the food bowls with vegetables and honey.

Some groups had villages with buildings. These well-established communities were built from stone, grass, mud, branches or even whalebones. You could change your house with the weather – there's no need for a roof in the dry season. But when the mozzies are out, then a raised platform or a windy spot is a good idea.

THE PALEO DIET

Aboriginal people arrived down-under in the Paleolithic period. There were no supermarkets here then. What did people eat? They stuck to the original Paleo diet. They ate just about any animal that moved, including turtles, snakes, possums, sugar-gliders, kangaroos and wombats. And emus, of course.

But that wasn't all. Australia is dry and hot in some areas, and cool and steamy in others. Inland and coastal people ate different foods, and saltwater people hunted at sea. Inland people enjoyed things you've probably never put on your plate. Which one of these treats would you choose from the menu?

- **Witchetty grubs** – one of these little wrigglers can give you as much protein as a pork chop.
- **Bogong moths** rest in huge swarms on rocks in the Snowy Mountains in NSW during summer. People came from all over to collect them and grill them on hot stones. They are very high in fat – like eating peanuts from the shell. They can also be ground up into moth butter.

- **Termites** – now we don't like these insects because they eat the wooden parts of houses. Perhaps this is revenge for all the termites that have been eaten by people.
- **Honey ants** – yes, they're sweet.
- **Daisy yam tubers** are dug out from the ground like potatoes.
- **Cycad fruit** will kill you if eaten raw. But women learned how to wash the poison out. They either left them in a stream for a week, or buried them until they fermented and frothed.
- **Bush tomatoes** grow on bushes in dry areas. They can be as big as a plum. They were left on the bushes to dry out and became a handy snack, like a prune or a sun-dried tomato.
- **Lerp** are soft, white spots found on gum leaves. They're very sugary. They were put in water to make cordial. Lerp is actually the cocoon excreted by insect larvae – in other words, a delicious baby insect poo.

SMART SURVIVAL TACTICS

Dinner wasn't always easy to catch and people used many tricks to nab their moving meals.

Think like a survivor: which method would you use for which animal?

HUNTING TRICKS

1 Blow a decoy horn that sounds like the female of this species, to attract males.

. . . .

2 Build a network of trenches and dirt banks, for water to flow through, slow and shallow, to trap the animal.

. . . .

3 String up a rope net over 50m long.

. . . .

4 Build a pen on the lake shore. Herd the babies of this species into the pen. Their mothers keep coming back to feed them. The babies keep healthy and growing, but they mysteriously disappear, one by one, as they get bigger and tastier.

. . . .

5 Put up a fence around a waterhole that forces your prey down a narrow corridor if it wants to drink, ready to be caught.

. . . .

6 Make the sound of a snake next to a burrow and this animal might come out.

. . . .

7 Make the sound of a hawk, so this animal will freeze on the spot.

. . . .

8 Climb into a tree and honk to bring this creature.

. . . .

HUNTED ANIMALS

A Geese
B Pelicans
C Emus
D Goannas

E Bandicoots
F Ducks
G Eels

Although people ate a lot of wild and wonderful things, communities had rules about food. Some foods were only for adults. In the Murrumbidgee area of NSW, only men were allowed to eat emu meat. If you were a Gagadju kid in the NT, flying fox was off the menu. Pregnant women in Arnhem Land in NT weren't allowed to eat fish caught with a line.

When somebody died in the Kimberley in WA, relatives weren't allowed to eat meat during the time of Sorry Business that followed, until elders said so.

WATER *SLEUTHS*

No one lasts long without water, so how did people get by in the desert?

Water was collected at waterholes and carried in bags sewn from kangaroo skin. A bag could hold up to 14 litres. That could last a family for a day or so. But if that ran out, there was water hidden in unexpected places.

- Find a casuarina, a kurrajong tree, a needle bush or some types of mallee scrub. Dig up a long root and break it off. Tip the water from the root into your mouth. Or see where a line of ants is marching to a hole in a tree. There will be water in there.

He's still following us!

- Stamp on the ground above a dried-up water-hole, so you sound like thunder. Any small frogs hibernating in the ground will think it's about to rain. When a frog starts to croak, dig it up. Squeeze it like a lemon so the water in its body runs out into your mouth.

- Follow a flock of zebra finches – they know where the water is.

HOW TO MAKE FIRE

On cold nights people needed heat and fire to cook, but there were no stoves, matches or lighters.

Here are some ways for a bright spark to get a fire going:

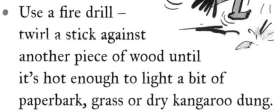

- Carry a firestick with you. In winter this is like holding your own personal heater.
- Use a fire drill – twirl a stick against another piece of wood until it's hot enough to light a bit of paperbark, grass or dry kangaroo dung.
- If you don't have a fire drill handy, use the edge of your woomera.
- Strike a piece of iron pyrite against stone to make sparks, which you can use to light grass, feathers or bark.

Woomera: a wooden spear-thrower.
Iron pyrite: a shiny mineral, also called 'fool's gold'.

SERIOUS SKILLS

Survival skills were passed down through the generations. The story of a WA man in the 1950s shows what was possible even in the toughest deserts of Australia.

A man named Jimmy Tjantjanu was arrested for stealing sheep. Then he was marched to a gaol on the coast. Despite being handcuffed, he escaped. He used fire sticks to light a fire and caught a large goanna. He caught two cats, ate one and kept the other for later. Then he walked over 800 kilometres, alone, for two months. That's about the distance between Melbourne and Sydney. It wasn't along a nice neat highway either – it was through difficult, dry desert country around a place called Sturt Creek in the Kimberley.

Tjantjanu didn't get caught. And he lived to tell his story after he found his way home without a map or compass.

This does not end well.

CULTURE COUNTRY

For thousands of years after the Ice Age, Aboriginal people survived and thrived. There were probably about 500 Aboriginal tribes here, speaking at least 250 different languages. Each group had its own culture and way of doing things.

Kids didn't go to school, but they had plenty to learn. Their teachers were their families and elders. Adult relatives were like extra mums and dads, who watched over them and told them what to do.

Kids learned stories that were science and history and music all rolled into one. The stories weren't just for fun. They were a database of information about animals and plants. And they passed on the Dreaming connection between people and country.

The land for us. No matter what
sort of animal, bird or snake,
all that animal same like us.
Our friend that.

Bill Neidje, Gagadju elder

BEWARE THE BUNYIP

Dreaming stories show how to look after the land, each other and yourself.

For example, the Ngarrindjeri in SA told their kids to beware of the Mulgewanki, who protected the Murray River.

He's half man and half fish.
He's got a lot of ribbon
weed on him. He's twice
the size of the average
man. He's a bit hairy and
furry with big red eyes,
big teeth, real sharp
claws, but also web hands,
feet like a duck and he's
the green brown colour of
the river. Don't go to the
water's edge by yourself

Mulgewanki: said 'Mool-ye-wonk'.

```
because you might fall in
and drown - the Mulgewanki's
going to get you.
```

Shane Karpany, Ngarrindjeri man

MUSICAL *MAPS*

Some stories were (and still are) told in songs and dances. A 'songline' is like a series about a journey by ancestor spirits. The Seven Sisters, for example, were chased by a man through the deserts of SA, WA and NT. The songs and stories about the Sisters describe those places. They make a kind of map, carried in people's heads.

```
The country is the text to
be read. Song is the means
to unravel the text.
```

Isabel Tarrago, Wangkamadla-Aranda woman,
from Simpson Desert country

Using these songs, people travelled a long way. Sometimes they carried valuable things for trading with other communities. In this way, pearl shells from the top of WA were swapped all the way down to the southern coast of Down Under.

ROCK STARS

Dreaming stories were also painted and carved onto rocks and shields.

Paint was made out of ochre. It came in different colours depending on what rock, clay or earth it was made from. There was white, red, yellow, green and brown, even a sparkly ochre from a rock called mica.

But if you've seen old rock paintings, you might have noticed that they're almost all red. That's because in hot dry weather the chemicals in other colours, especially yellow and brown, are eventually cooked and turn red.

Rock art painters didn't sign their name like Picasso. But some of them did leave a kind of signature. They made hand stencils, by putting their hand on the rock face and spraying paint around it from their mouth.

SECRET *CEREMONIES*

Ochre could be used for bodies too. Especially when people got together to sing, dance and do ceremonies. If you were a boy becoming a man, you didn't have a birthday party, but you did have a ceremony to mark the occasion.

In NSW, the ceremonies involved knocking out a front tooth. In Queensland and SA, you'd get long scars cut into your back. You learned things you couldn't share with anyone in another community, or even your mother or sister.

Girls had ceremonies too and they were also very secret. On the upside, your mum wouldn't have shared embarrassing photos of you on Facebook – even if it had been invented.

Ceremonies: a formal event with set actions, like a graduation or a wedding.

SILENT *SPEAKING*

Many communities 'talked' in sign languages as well as spoken languages. It was useful when you needed to communicate silently, like when you were hunting. Or if you met someone from a different language group.

These are signs used in Queensland. Can you guess what each one means?

HAND-SIGNS

1. Claw downwards with two fingers.

. . . .

2. Cup hands below your jaw.

. . . .

3. Blow into your hand.

. . . .

4. Stick out your bottom lip and pat it with two fingers.

. . . .

5. With forefinger curved, flick your wrist outwards.

. . . .

6. Draw small circle in the air.

. . . .

7. Point your finger out from your nose.

. . . .

8. Tap your shoulder (where things are carried).

. . . .

⑨ Touch behind your ear.

⑩ Curl your fingers down, hop your hands forward.

⑪ Point your forefinger and little finger.

⑫ Bite your beard or the top of your thumb.

MEANING

Ⓐ Fire

Ⓑ Child

Ⓒ Brother or sister

Ⓓ Possum

Ⓔ Baby

Ⓕ Pelican

Ⓖ Pituri (desert tobacco)

Ⓗ Bad person or thing

Ⓘ Kangaroo

Ⓙ Anger

Ⓚ Bandicoot

Ⓛ Boomerang

Bad person or thing

Rock 'n' Roll

55

FARMING WITH FIRE

Aboriginal people cared for and farmed their country. They were experts in using plants and animals to make what they needed. They were also experts in using a powerful and dangerous tool – fire.

By setting fire to the bush, it didn't get too thick. Instead of tangly bushes, more grass grew. That was nice for the kangaroos to eat, but also nice for the men who hunted them.

Aboriginal women put plant roots back in the ground after taking some to eat. That way more would grow for next time. People also made wooden dishes or skin bags to keep seeds, then hid them in the ground. The biggest stash ever found had almost a tonne of seed (about the same weight as a small flock of 10–20 sheep). When food is precious, that's a big hoard of buried treasure.

ANCIENT FISH FARMS

In southwest Victoria there are networks of stone walls first built 6600 years ago. The walls were built around and through water. They look like a maze, but they're not – unless you're an eel.

The walls funnelled the eels into ponds where they were stuck. At least until a hungry Gunditjmara family came along and fished out a few for dinner.

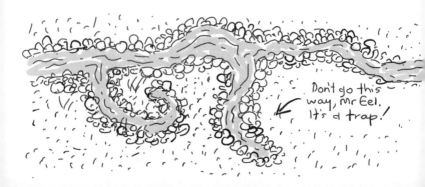

Don't go this way, mr Eel. It's a trap!

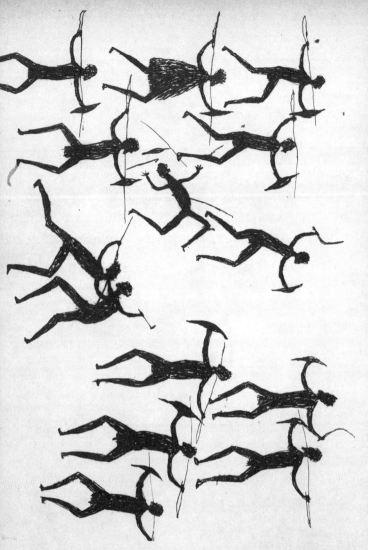

Weapons weren't always used for hunting food. They were sometimes used against people. In this picture, of 'Two Aboriginal Tribes fighting', you can see the men using boomerangs, spear-throwers, shields and an axe. It was drawn by Yorta Yorta man Tommy McRae in 1881, near the Murray River in Victoria.

WEAPONS *KNOW-HOW*

Boys learned to make weapons from stone and wood – axes, spears, spear-throwers, shields and boomerangs.

Can you pass this weapons test with flying colours?

1. **Boomerangs are unique to Australia**

   ☐ True ☐ False

2. **Boomerangs always come back**

   ☐ True ☐ False

3. **Boomerangs were toys for boys**

   ☐ True ☐ False

4. **Australia's biggest rocket-launch range is named after the Dharug word for a spear-thrower**

   ☐ True ☐ False

5. **In 1770, Captain Cook thought Dharug boomerangs were curved swords**

   ☐ True ☐ False

Answers: 1 False – Ancient Egyptians had similar weapons, 2 False – some are not designed to come back, 3 False – they were used by men as tools and weapons, 4 True – Woomera, 5 True

FABULOUS *FASHIONS*

Aboriginal people were not embarrassed about naked bodies then, like we are now. But they did wear clothes sometimes, to keep warm or protect their bodies.

NEW SEASON'S KANGAROO SKIN OUTFIT FOR THE NEW MOTHER

← Special pouch for the baby

Desert people made sandals from bark and grass to protect their feet. And a fur cloak, now in a museum in Victoria, is sewn from the skins of 81 possums. Heavy, but very cosy!

Torres Strait Islanders made beautiful head-dresses for ceremonies and dances called Dharis or Dhoeris. People also made jewellery from bird feathers, animal teeth and skulls. Fancy a snake skeleton as a necklace?

That coat is like our family photo album

DOWNSIDES OF *DOWN UNDER*

The good old days were not always good. It was tough living without all the things we take for granted now.

Back then you would not have lasted long if:

- You were disabled so you couldn't hunt or gather food.
- You were born a twin, or close in age to your older brother or sister, as your mother couldn't carry you both – there were no prams in the Simpson desert or the Snowy Mountains.
- Your mother died and there wasn't anyone else to breastfeed and carry you – there was no milk-powder or baby food.
- You were sick or elderly and couldn't keep up.

If you survived, here are some things you may not have enjoyed:

- Girls were married before they were grown up and usually to older men. If a girl ran away to be with a boy she loved, she could be hunted down and killed.
- Women were supposed to do what men told them.

- Men were allowed to give a wife to someone else, or sell her for pituri or other valuable items.

Aboriginal communities had some extreme ways of unfriending each other.

- Medicine men were believed to heal people and make rain. But they also cursed people. A sorcerer made a magical pointing bone. When he pointed the bone at someone, even from far off, that person got sick. If the medicine man heated or burnt the bone, the victim got worse and died.
- When a person died of illness or accident, their family often tried to work out who was to blame. For example, a Ngarrindjeri relative in SA might sleep with their head on the dead body. If they dreamed of someone, he or she was the murderer. Sometimes this would lead to a revenge attack on the person or even the person's community.

If that sounds tough, there was worse to come. Because millions of years after Australia had drifted away from the rest of the world, and 65,000 years or more after people had first come to its shores, the land down-under was eventually found by someone else ...

HIT AND MISS

A few hundred years ago the oceans around the land down-under got a lot busier. A few hundred years was the blink of an eye for this ancient land. But sometimes a lot can happen in the blink of an eye.

Around 400 years ago, the neighbours, from Macassar in Indonesia, began dropping in to the land they called 'Marege'.

The Macassans started to visit Marege every year. Up to a thousand Macassans would sail over in ships called 'praus', armed with daggers, muskets and even cannon.

They weren't coming for a fight, though. They came for a small, slimy sea slug called trepang or sea cucumber.

FOOD TOURISTS

Here's how to make trepang:

* Translated from the Macassan

- Dive to collect the trepang from underwater, then boil it in a pan of mangrove bark.
- Dry it out and bury it in some sand, then dig it up and boil it again.
- Smoke it over a low fire in a smokehouse made of bamboo.

> Sea cucumber is tasteless, full of sand and stinky – the most difficult thing to cook.
>
> Chinese cookbook
> *Recipes from the Sui Garden*, 1792

Sounds gross, doesn't it? The result was 'like sausages which have been rolled in mud and then thrown up the chimney', according to an Englishman. Not very delicious perhaps. But many people in China and Southeast Asia believe it's good for you, like a kind of medicine.

The Macassans also went home with turtle shells, pearls, and (mostly) the friendship of the Aboriginal people of the north coast.

In return they left metal tools, nails, the idea of dugout canoes, words from the Macassan language, a fashion for pointy beards and some babies the men had with local women. These things were important and valuable. Especially if you happened to be one of the babies. The Macassans kept visiting right up until the late 1880s. But they didn't disturb life too much. They came, they traded and they went. The main losers were the sea cucumbers.

THE UNKNOWN LAND

Far, far away in Europe, people had worked out how to build better weapons and better ships. By the sixteenth century, they were armed with guns. They got more adventurous. And even more interested in other people's stuff.

Europeans had a hunch that the land down-under existed. But only because an Ancient Greek called Aristotle had decided the world should have something on the other side. He thought

There has to be something down-under!

the world was flat and that it would tip over if it wasn't balanced.

Another ancient thinker took up the idea and drew a map with this land on it. He called it Terra Australis Incognita – the Unknown South Land.

This lucky guess was about to become very unlucky for the first people of Australia.

SHARE NICELY, PLEASE

In 1488 a Portuguese sailor, Bartholomew Diaz, became the first European captain to sail around the bottom of Africa.

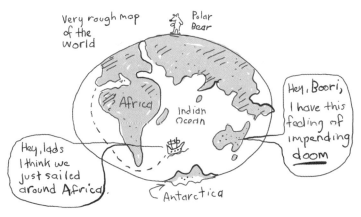

This brought Europeans into new waters and a lot closer to the mysterious Terra Australis Incognita. But they hadn't spotted it yet.

Still, their trip opened new opportunities.

A couple of years later, the Pope kindly agreed that the world outside Europe could be divided in half. Portugal could have one half, he said, and Spain could have the other.

The Pope thought he represented God. So he didn't ask anyone's opinion on this decision – certainly not the people of Asia, Africa and the Americas.

ARE WE THERE YET?

European explorers bravely sailed off into a vast, scary blank on the world map. They had no GPS to tell them where they were or how to get home.

Sailors used the sun and stars to work out their north–south position. But even these looked different on the other side of the world.

> A marvellous cross in the midst of five notable stars which compass it about ... This cross is so fair and beautiful that none other heavenly sign may be compared to it.
>
> A Portuguese adventurer describing the Southern Cross, 1515

Figuring out their east–west position was very difficult. It was a huge breakthrough when a clock that worked at sea was invented in the late 1700s. This made measuring much more accurate.

KNOT WHAT YOU THINK

Sailing ships were complicated and expensive pieces of technology. They were pre-modern rocket science. Can you work out what each of these ship-bits are called?

SHIP SHAPE SHIP-BITS

1 Where luggage and goods are kept

. . . .

Luggage

2 Tool for measuring the angle of the sun, moon and stars

. . . .

3 Stones used to balance a ship

. . . .

4 To overturn in water

. . . .

5 Where sailors sleep

. . . .

stones

6 How fast a ship is travelling

7 Ropes

8 How much a ship can carry

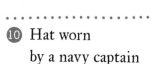

9 The third mast

10 Hat worn by a navy captain

11 The highest deck on a ship

Augh!

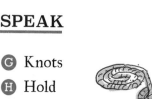

SAILOR SPEAK

A Poop

B Sextant

C Tons

D Ballast

E Sheets

F Mizzen

G Knots

H Hold

I Tricorn

J Capsize

K Forecastle or fo'c'sle

THE (UN)LUCKY LAND OF LUCA

Portuguese merchants took as much as they could from their half of the world. Big money was to be made from spices like nutmeg and pepper. Plenty of these grew in our neighbourhood, which the Europeans called the East Indies.

In about 1601, a Portuguese adventurer called Manuel Godinho de Erédia heard a rumour. An Indonesian king boasted that he had visited 'Luca Antara', a place south of Timor. His 'eyewitness' reports sounded fabulous. The land was full of gold and spices, and the people spent all their time playing sport and wore golden crowns on their heads.

Sounds too good to be true, perhaps? Well, the King of Portugal sent Erédia to check it out anyway. Erédia started travelling in the right direction, but then he got stuck in Malaysia. The Malays attacked the Portuguese fortress he was staying in, so he decided to hang out and inflict 'much damage on the villages' of Malaysia for a bit.

After that nasty job was done, he was going to set out for Luca Antara again. But he got sick with a disease called beriberi, which causes swollen legs, paralysis and brain damage.

Erédia was forced to give up exploring, which was probably just as well, because his maps and directions were very confused. He and his crew would probably have ended up very lost.

BATTLE *SHIPS*

Portugal was not the only European country good at building ships or interested in making money. In 1602, the Dutch started a company called the East India Company. Their fleet of ships didn't just trade, they also fought.

They beat the Portuguese fleet in 1606 in two furious sea battles. Twelve ships were sunk, some set alight by their own cannon-fire. Ten of them were Portuguese.

```
You English should never sneer
at the Dutch or Spanish - they
were before you everywhere.
```

English writer Henry Kingsley, in an 1859 novel

Fleet: a group of ships sailing together.

So the Dutch got the run of the south seas. It wasn't long before they ran into the land down-under.

THE LANDING OF THE DOVE

The East India Company sent one of its ships south from Indonesia to find new places to make money. The ship was under the command of Captain Willem Jansz.

It was called the *Duyfken*, meaning 'Little Dove', perhaps because it was only 20 metres long (the length of four or five cars end to end).

The Little Dove sailed through the Torres Strait and came to rest on the northern tip of Australia on 26 February 1606. Jansz and some of his men went ashore. There they met some of the local Wik people.

It was the first known meeting between Aboriginal people and Europeans.

The meeting did not go well.

Dutch and Aboriginal versions of the story are different. The Dutch said they just wanted to trade, but the locals attacked. The Wik say they welcomed the men from the 'big mob of logs', but the foreigners stole two women. Everyone agrees that the result was deaths on both sides.

The Little Dove took off, back along the coast of what the captain (wrongly) thought was New Guinea.

ROARING *ALONG*

In 1610 a Dutch explorer, Hendrik Brouwer, discovered a new way of sailing to the East Indies. Instead of going round the bottom of Africa and back up along its east coast, he sailed straight south from the Cape and turned east. There his ship caught the 'Roaring Forties'. No, they're not a disease or a rock band. They're strong winds, named after their usual position 40 degrees south of the equator on the globe.

If you go even further south you find yourself in the Furious Fifties and Screaming Sixties.

Taking the Roaring Forties made the trip much faster. Sometimes too fast. If a captain didn't change direction in time, then the wind would blow him straight into the coast of WA.

That's what happened to a series of ships.

The first was the *Eendracht* in 1616. The ship's captain, Dirk Hartog, came ashore on WA's largest island. He named the country 'Landt van de Eendracht', after his ship. He also nailed a dinner plate to a tree. In those days good plates were made of metal, so that's not quite as strange as it sounds. The plate was inscribed: *On the 25th of October 1616, arrived here the ship Eendracht, of Amsterdam.*

It was the beginning of a long tradition of Europeans coming down-under and naming stuff after themselves. The local people, who already had a name for their home and didn't need dinner plates, must have wondered what he was doing.

who are you?
whatcha doing?
Are you an alien?

THE TRIALS OF THE TRYALL

In 1622 a man called John Brookes was made captain of a new English ship. It was called the *Tryall* – not a hopeful name, as 'trial' can also mean a tough experience.

Captain Brookes was supposed to sail to the East Indies using Brouwer's 'Roaring Forties' route. The *Tryall* was brand-new, but the captain and his officers were too. None of them had ever been to the East Indies.

Thinking they were in the middle of the ocean, the newbie crew imagined they were doing fine. The captain didn't bother to put anyone on lookout. In the middle of the night, the ship smashed into rocks. Brookes had almost sailed straight into the west coast of Down Under.

```
Ye rock being sharpe, ye ship
was presentlie full of water.
```

Captain John Brookes,
report to the East India Company, 1622

Brookes ordered his crew to move supplies into two small rowing boats. It took them hours. The ship began to break up. He promised he would try to rescue them all. But while most of the crew weren't looking, he took the smallest boat, along with 10 men and the ship's silver. Then 36 others squashed into the second rowboat. Brookes left 93 sailors behind on the sinking ship.

Amazingly, both rowboats made it all the way to Indonesia, 1800 kilometres away. Nobody knows what happened to the 93 left behind. But we can guess.

THE BAD BATAVIA

If you think the wreck of the *Tryall* was bad, the story of the *Batavia* is worse. In 1629, this Dutch ship crashed into a reef down-under in the dark.

The ship had an impressive stash of cash on board – $20 million in today's money. But the man in command of this ship, Francisco Pelsaert, decided to save the 330 people on board instead. He managed to get most of them onto a nearby island.

He then set out on a sturdy longboat to look for

water. A group of more than 40 people, including the senior officers, were with him. When they didn't find any water, they decided they might as well keep going and get help from the Dutch East Indies. It was an almost impossible journey, but everyone survived.

Meanwhile, back on the island, a man named Jeronimus Cornelisz had taken charge. He dressed up in crimson robes with gold lace, taken from the wreck. At first, anyone against him was killed by order of a 'council'. But after a while, Cornelisz and his supporters started openly murdering people – even women and children, and a baby who cried too much.

A group of men escaped to another island, which had animals to eat and fresh water. Cornelisz and his supporters came to attack them. The men fought back. Just as an all-out battle was beginning, a ship was sighted. It was Pelsaert, come back on a rescue mission. In the three months he had been

They went to the main city of the **Dutch East Indies**, which was also (confusingly) called Batavia – *that* Batavia is now Jakarta, capital of Indonesia.

gone, at least 115 people had been murdered. Only about 70 made it safely to the East Indies.

The ship itself was finally rescued from the bottom of the ocean more than three centuries later, along with some of the treasure. You can see a large piece of the Batavia in a museum in Fremantle, WA. The stone fort ruins on the island are the oldest European buildings in Australia.

MYSTERY SHIPS

We know about the *Tryall* and *Batavia* because some people got home to tell the tale. Other crews never made it. Around the coast of Australia are clues to more accidental arrivals.

- A very old Spanish sailor's knife was found in a swamp in the 1930s on Stradbroke Island off the coast of Queensland. An English coin dated 1597 was found in 2007. The top of a walking stick, shaped like a man's head with a seventeenth-century hairstyle, also turned up nearby.
- Ancient coins have been found on an island off the coast of NT. Five of them were copper coins from an African kingdom in the tenth century. In the same spot were

four Dutch coins from the seventeenth
and eighteenth centuries.

- Newspapers in 1847 reported an ancient
mahogany ship on a Victorian beach. It has
since disappeared.

NEAR *MISSES*

Australia is a huge continent, but so many sailors
managed to miss it or didn't realise what they'd
found. It was almost as if Terra Incognita was still
on the move, playing hide and seek.

- **1567** The Spanish ruler of Peru sent his
nephew, Álvaro de Mendaña, to discover
Terra Australis. Mendaña got to the Solomon
Islands instead.
- **1606** Pedro de Queirós, a Portuguese navigator working for Spain, landed three ships
on a coast that he proclaimed to be 'La
Austrialia del Espiritu Santo'. It was actually
Vanuatu.
- **1606** Queirós' ship went missing in bad
weather. One of his deputies, Luis de Torres,
sailed another ship along the coast of New
Guinea searching for him. Torres spotted 'very
large islands, and more to the south' but didn't

realise he'd found what the others had been looking for all along.

- **1642** Searching for the fabulous gold of a place called 'Beach', the Dutch explorer Abel Tasman sailed around Tasmania, which he called 'Van Diemen's Land'. But after his ship was damaged in a storm, he went east, missed the mainland and found New Zealand.
- Tasman came back in **1644** and mapped the north coast of Australia. He certainly found some beaches, but no gold.
- **1699** English pirate William Dampier sailed 1000km along the north-west coast of 'New Holland', now WA. Dampier wanted to find the east coast but had to turn back because he couldn't find fresh water.
- **1768** The French explorer Louis de Bougainville got so close to the coast of Queensland that he could see waves breaking on rocks. But his crew were already so hungry they were eating leather parts from the ship – he turned away from the dangerous reef and didn't find Australia.

So Down Under stayed 'incognita' for centuries. Aboriginal people went on with their daily lives while European ships explored the coasts around them.

TERRA INCOGNITA

WHAT AUSTRALIA WAS NEARLY CALLED

If things had gone differently, we might not be calling our country Australia at all. We could be living in:

- **Terra Australis Incognita**
  Meaning 'Unknown southern land'
- **Marege** The Macassan name for northern Australia
- **Jave La Grande** Meaning 'Big Java', found on some early French maps
- **The Antipodes** Meaning 'Opposite feet' in Latin, first used in Europe in 1398 to mean the other side of the world
- **Luca Antara** One of Erédia's names for the southern lands
- **Meridional India** Another of Erédia's names

- **Boesche** Meaning 'Beach', possibly a wrong translation of 'Lochac', a place described by the Italian traveller Marco Polo
- **La Austrialia del Espiritu Santo** What Querós was planning to call Terra Australis, named after Austria, where the Spanish royal family came from
- **Landt van de Eendracht** Meaning 'Land of the *Eendracht*', named after Hartog's ship
- **Hollandia Nova** or **Nieuw Hollande** Meaning 'New Holland'; found on Dutch maps of WA
- **Terre Napoleon** The French explorer Nicolas Baudin's name for southern Australia in 1802
- **Terra Australis** The name preferred by the English explorer Joseph Banks
- **New South Wales** English explorer Captain Cook's name for the whole eastern side of Down Under

From henceforth this great southern land will be khown as.... um...
Marege! ... um... no!
.. erh... **Jave la Grande**
um ...

AUSTRALIA!

COOK TAKES A LOOK

It took a long while for Europeans to find the mysterious land down-under partly because sailing was dangerous and difficult. But it was also because maps were top secret. Companies and countries didn't want their competitors to have such useful information. Sailors were forbidden 'on pain of death' to copy maps or tell foreigners about them. Clearly it didn't occur to them to ask the Macassans for directions.

Sometimes information leaked out. Torres' report on his trip past Australia was captured when the British defeated Spain in the Philippines in 1762. Britain had picked this fight as part of a war back in Europe, which they also won – the Torres report was just a bonus.

SECRET SCIENCE BUSINESS

One Englishman who saw Torres' secret information was a member of the Royal Society – an English club for rich men interested in science.

The Society planned to send a ship full of gentlemen scientists, the *Endeavour*, to the south seas in 1769. They wanted to time how long it took for the planet Venus to cross in front of the sun (this only happens twice a century). Then they could work out how far the Earth is from our star, the sun.

But there was a second, secret set of instructions for the trip. The captain of the ship, James Cook, was instructed to 'proceed to the southward in order to make discovery of the Continent'.

You are to carefully observe the Nature of the Soil, and the Products thereof. In case you find any Mines, Minerals or valuable stones you are to bring home Specimens of each, as also such Specimens of the Seeds of the Trees.

Additional Instructions
to Captain James Cook, 1768

Britain was after gold and spices, too.

There was to be no sugar and spice for this Cook, and no gold, but he did find Terra Australis Incognita, the Unknown Southern Land.

HOW COOK NEARLY SANK

Cook was an excellent navigator and by April 1770, the ship *Endeavour* had landed at a place he called Botany Bay. By June, they were sailing along the Great Barrier Reef while Cook did a thorough job of mapping the east coast of Australia.

Cook was feeling pretty pleased with himself. And so was Joseph Banks, one of the scientists on board. They had filled the ship with a pile of unique plant and animal specimens.

```
I have made no great
discoveries yet I have
explored more of the Great
South Sea than all that have
gone before me.
```

Captain James Cook, 1771

But Cook was taking a huge risk sailing so close to the coast. On 11 June, just as everyone was going to bed, the ship hit the reef.

The hull got stuck. Cook's crew threw everything heavy overboard. That included cannons, old stores and ballast. They even took down part of the masts, to make the ship lighter.

Cook hoped that the ship would lift off the reef at high tide.

It didn't.

Luckily the sea was calm, so the waves didn't grind the bottom of the ship against the reef. But as the tide went out again the ship began to tilt and let in water. Everyone took turns on the pumps, including the officers and gentlemen like Banks.

If the ship went down, all its equipment and supplies would sink. If the crew didn't drown, they would be washed up down-under forever. You might think there are worse places than Queensland to be stuck on permanent holiday, but there were no resorts or caravan parks there then.

Hull: the main body of a ship.

> This was a terrible circumstance and threatened immediate destruction to us.

At the next high tide, water might come pouring in too fast to pump out. The ship could sink. The situation was so serious that the sailors apparently even stopped swearing. As the tide came up, the ship moved. By sheer luck, the piece of coral poking into the hull broke off and plugged the hole. The *Endeavour* was pulled off the reef by rowboats.

The crew then 'fothered' the ship – volunteers swam underneath and put a sail smeared with sheep poo against the hull. The giant poopy bandage worked. Cook was able to sail the ship in to the beach for his carpenters to fix.

The crew only got a month's holiday by the beach, instead of a lifetime.

If the *Endeavour* had not made it back, the east coast would have stayed off British maps. The people of Australia might have been left in peace for a little while longer, or they might have seen more of the French or the Dutch.

But on 22 August 1770, just before he left for home, Cook hoisted the English flag on an island off the coast.

'In the Name of His Majesty King George the Third,' he said, 'I took possession of the whole Eastern Coast ... by the name of New South Wales.'

The Aboriginal people knew nothing about this new name, of course. The square of coloured cloth probably fluttered for a while then rotted away. But it wasn't the last they would see of the British.

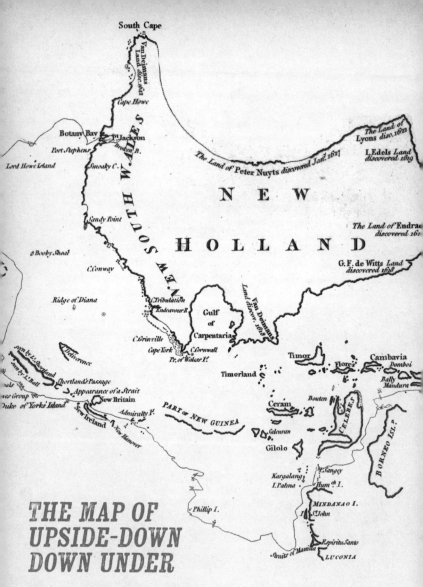

South Cape

Van Diemans Land disc. 1612

Cape Howe

Botany Bay

Pt. Jackson

Port Stephens

Broken B.

Lord Howe Island

Smoaky C.

NEW SOUTH WALES

Sandy Point

S. Booby Shoal

C. Conway

Ridge of Diana

C. Tribulation

Endeavour R.

C. Grinville

Cape York

C. Cornwall

Pr. of Wales I.

The Land of Lyons disc. 1622

I. Edels Land discovered 1619

The Land of Peter Nuyts discovered Jan. 1627

N E W

H O L L A N D

The Land of Endra discovered 161

G. F. de Witts Land discovered 1628

Gulf of Carpentaria

Van Diemans Land disc. 1618

Timor

Timorland

Flores

Cambavia

Donboi

Bally

Mandura

seen by Lt. Shortland

seen by L. Ball

Shortland's Passage

Appearance of a Strait

New Britain

Duke of Yorks Island

Deliverance

Admiralty I.

New Ireland

New Hanover

PART OF NEW GUINEA

Ceram

Bouten

Galeran

Gilolo

Kargalang

I. Palma

S. Sangey

Hum I.

CELEBES

BORNEO ISL.?

Phillip I.

MINDANAO I.

St. John

E. Spiritu Santo

Straits of Manilla

LUCONIA

THE MAP OF UPSIDE-DOWN DOWN UNDER

This is a chart showing the journey of a transport
ship from Port Jackson in New South Wales to Batavia
in Indonesia. This is how Australia looked from an
English angle in 1792. The coastline is fairly accurate,
but it's not *quite* what we're used to seeing…

FIRST IMPRESSIONS

The Europeans who visited Australia were considered great scientists. They wrote about what they saw in diaries and books, which were the eighteenth century version of online reviews. But they didn't give too many 'likes'.

Joseph Banks said that Botany Bay in NSW looked like 'the back of a lean cow ... the most barren country I have seen'.

Captain Cook wrote that 'the natives of New Holland may appear to be some of the most wretched people upon Earth'. These days it is insulting to call someone a 'native', let alone say their lifestyle is 'wretched'.

The Dutch East India Company reported that they 'found everywhere shallow water and barren coast; islands altogether thinly peopled by various cruel, poor and brutal nations'. They sound very unimpressed by both the land down-under and its people.

Most Europeans believed their own countries were technologically advanced and therefore better.

> There never was any
> civilized nation of
> any other complexion
> than white.

David Hume, Scottish philosopher, 1742

It was true that Europe had guns, factories and tall buildings. But it also had rats, raw sewage and starvation.

To be fair to Captain Cook, he also wrote that Aboriginal people were 'far happier than we Europeans ... The earth and sea furnishes them with all things necessary for life.'

One of the biggest differences the Europeans noticed was that there were no fences that they could see. In European thinking, if you didn't have fences, you didn't own the place. The British saw the land down-under as theirs to take.

A DIFFERENT COUNTRY

In Aboriginal thinking, that wasn't the case at all. Woollarawarre Bennelong, an Eora man from NSW, told the Englishman David Collins in 1790 that 'the island Me-mel close by Sydney Cove was his property; that it was his father's'. He also told Collins that other Eora had this kind of property too. He was probably proud of his country, and didn't think it was barren at all.

Aboriginal people weren't all that impressed with the European way of life either.

One of the first Eora men to meet the English, Arabanoo, thought that alcohol was disgusting. And Bennelong's wife, Barangaroo, was so horrified when she saw a flogging that she grabbed the whip out of the flogger's hands.

Unfortunately, Europeans thought so little of Aboriginal opinions that very few of them were written down.

Flogging: beating someone with a whip – a common punishment in the British army and navy at the time.

UPSIDE-DOWN, *BACK TO FRONT*

The more the British got to know the land down-under, the stranger they would find it.

> There is a place
>   in distant seas
> Full of contrarieties;
> There parrots walk
>   upon the ground
> And grass upon the
>   trees is found
> There birds although
>   they cannot fly
> In swiftness with
>   your greyhound vie
> Now of what place could
>   such strange tales
> Be told with truth
>   save New South Wales?

From a poem by Englishman
Richard Whately, 1846

Everything seemed upside-down. The British felt like nature was playing a giant joke on them. The seasons were opposite to the northern half of the world. River beds had no water in them. Trees dropped their bark more than their leaves. Here the swans were black instead of white. Mice could fly – at least that's what Europeans thought about feathertail gliders. Kangaroos looked like no other animal and carried their young in a pouch on their front.

One of Cook's sailors saw a big bat and thought it was the Devil. The terrified man reported that it was 'as large as a one gallon keg, and ... had horns and wings'.

WEIRD AND WONDERFUL

One animal that really stumped European scientists was the platypus. They couldn't work out whether it was a duck, a turtle or a mammal. Some of them didn't believe it was real. They thought the stuffed platypuses brought back to Europe were fakes.

The platypus's rear end, with only one opening for poo and reproduction, was too embarrassing to describe.

And what of this creature's bottom, Jeremiah?

There'll be no mention of that part, Wilfred!

> It appears to possess
> a threefold nature, that of a
> fish, a bird, and a quadruped,
> and is related to nothing we
> have hitherto seen.

Thomas Bewick, natural history author, 1800

And all this amazement was before they worked out that platypuses lay eggs (which wasn't until 1884).

Australian animals actually have even stranger secrets that Europeans didn't find out for a long time. How much do *you* know about our native animals?

Ⓐ When do male antechinuses die?
(An antechinus is a marsupial that looks like a mouse.)

Ⓑ What do young koalas eat before they can digest leaves?

As one of Australia's first scientific organisations said: in the land down-under 'All things are queer and opposite'.

Answers: A After mating to produce young. That way there's more food to go around when the babies are born. **B** Baby koalas eat a 'pap' – a special pellet full of useful bacteria that is pooed out for them by their mother.

THE GIANT GARBAGE DUMP

Over in Europe, society was changing. Scientists were busy discovering and inventing. Their new machines took over people's old jobs. In Britain, new laws let the rich fence in land that once belonged to everybody.

Thousands of desperate people crowded into cities all over Europe. Some got jobs in the new factories. About half the workers were children. They worked 10–18 hours a day, but many families still didn't have enough to live on.

England's biggest city, London, got bigger, dirtier and more dangerous. The city's population topped one million.

Britain: included England, Scotland and Wales – also Ireland from 1800 to 1922, although the Irish did not agree with this at all!

All sorts of people took to a life of crime just to survive. The man who started Britain's first police force said, in 1797, that up to 115,000 Londoners made their living illegally.

What did the British government do about this? It didn't fix the problems, it made the laws tougher.

CRIMES TO DIE FOR

The worst punishment was death. Even children could be executed.

By the early 1800s there were nearly 250 crimes you could die for. They were called 'capital offences'. 'Capital' is from the Latin word for 'head', because that's what it cost you. The judge would order that you be 'hanged by the neck until dead'.

A condemned criminal climbed up a wooden platform, had a rope put around their neck and then 'swung' by the rope.

Minor crimes had major consequences. You could be killed for:

- Pretending you were a gypsy
- Trapping a rabbit on land that wasn't yours

- 'Stealing' an heiress (kidnapping and marrying a young woman with a lot of money)
- Being on a highway with your face blackened
- Setting fire to a haystack
- Stealing a sheep or cow
- Stealing mail
- Faking money or documents

See if you can guess which is the odd crime out.

Which of these was NOT a capital offence?

Ⓐ Stealing anything worth more than five shillings (the cost of a pair of stockings)

Ⓑ 'Strong evidence of malice' in a child 7–14 years old

Ⓒ Kidnapping a child

Ⓓ Setting fire to a haystack

Ⓔ Fighting a duel

During the 1770s, more than a thousand people were found guilty of capital crimes in just the London area – 531 of them were executed.

Answer: C That's right, children aged 7–14 could be hanged but not child kidnappers. Although to be fair, the kidnappers usually stole the clothes from rich kids then let the child go.

MAKING FUN OF DEATH

Hanging people wasn't just a way of getting rid of criminals. Executions were supposed to scare everyone else into good behaviour. And to do that they had to be public. Death became entertainment. Tens of thousands of people came to watch each 'event'.

> Executions are intended to draw spectators. If they do not draw spectators they do not answer to their purpose.
>
> English writer Samuel Johnson, 1783

English people had different names for hanging:

- Dance the Paddington frisk
- Be in deadly suspense
- Dance upon nothing
- Have a hearty choke with caper sauce
- Go up the ladder to bed
- Take a leap in the dark
- Poke your tongue out at the company
- Climb the Nevergreen tree that bears fruit all year round

CRAMMED *CRIMS*

Many judges were not as mean as the laws. They didn't want to kill people for crimes like stealing.

By the end of the 1700s, less than one fifth of condemned criminals in England were actually hanged. So the prisons became crowded with convicts.

Prisons were run like a kind of zoo – sightseers were allowed in to stare at people who were mentally ill or so poor they were half-naked.

The visitors are coming, time to put on a show.

Can I be the naked mad man today?

Dead rat on a plate

Convicts: criminals who had been 'convicted', meaning found guilty of a crime.

Sightseers, visitors and even the convicts were charged an entrance fee, and convicts had to buy their own food. When the keeper of Newgate Prison died in 1792, he had made a fortune of £20,000, which would be something like $5 million today.

> The roaring, swearing and clamour, the stench and nastiness, joined together to make the place seem an emblem of hell itself.
>
> Moll Flanders describes Newgate Prison, from the novel by Daniel Defoe, 1722

Sometimes prison was a death sentence of its own. It wasn't other criminals who were the greatest threat. It was dirt and disease. More prisoners died of 'gaol fever' than of hanging, a report said in 1784. Not many people cared much if the poor died.

INCREDIBLE HULKS

In England, the prisons got so full, the government began storing people on old ships.

These broken and rotten boats were called 'hulks' and they were run by businessmen who wanted to make as much money as possible.

£: said 'pound', English money, which was later used in colonial Australia.

A visitor in 1778 noted that the convicts had no bedding. The biscuits they had to eat were all 'mouldy and green on both sides'. Even the owners admitted that up to a third of hulk prisoners died on board.

SHIPPED *OUT*

The British government decided to send some of their criminals away instead. Thousands of them were shipped to America, which had been an English colony since the 1600s.

After a while the Americans got tired of taking Britain's convicts. They wanted liberty and freedom for themselves (although not for their African slaves). They complained that 'America has been made the very common sewer and dung yard to Britain' – or, in other words, Britain was using America as a toilet.

The Americans were so tired of British behaviour that they successfully fought a War of Independence between 1775 and 1783 to get rid of them. The lid was shut on that 'sewer', and Britain had to look elsewhere.

Colony: a place settled and controlled by another country.

COLONY BY COMMITTEE

The British government put together a committee to solve the problem. They called in Joseph Banks for a chat. Remember how Banks had called Australia 'the most barren country' he had ever seen? He seems to have had a short memory. This time he recommended that Britain send a large number of people to Botany Bay.

He told them:

- It was seven months by ship from England so the convicts couldn't escape.
- There was hardly anybody else there.
- The weather was mild and moderate.
- There were no beasts of prey, and plenty of grass for cows and sheep.
- There was fish to eat, a good supply of water and timber for buildings, so the criminals could look after themselves, without help from Britain.

Barren, empty, no takeaway shops, nothing!!

He also suggested that the continent was so big that there must be profit in it somewhere for Britain if they started a colony there. Most of what he told them about the land down-under was, well, imaginative. But it was what the committee wanted to hear.

MORE BOAT PEOPLE

In 1787, a navy captain was given the job of putting out Britain's human rubbish.

Captain Arthur Phillip had been a sailor since he was 15. He spoke several languages and had spent time spying on Britain's enemies, the French and Portuguese, and fighting against them. This mission was even more adventurous. He was to take 11 ships and nearly 1500 people to the other side of the world and set up a colony.

The British government wanted to do it on the cheap. Luckily for the convicts and the others on the ships, Phillip was very organised and forward-thinking. He wrote letter after letter, pestering the government to think about pesky details, like clothes, nails, medical supplies and rules.

WHAT TO PACK?

In May 1787 the ships set sail for Australia. It wasn't called that yet, of course. In Europe it was still called New Holland. The plan was to desert the convicts eventually, with 'no hope of returning' as the King of Great Britain – King George III – put it.

If you were going, what would you take? Phillip took:

- Enough food to last two years
- Fish hooks
- Door hinges
- Cows, horses, 70 sheep, geese
- 8 cannon
- 5000 bricks
- Seeds for coffee
- Seeds of indigo plants for dying clothes blue
- Ginger roots
- A special seal for the captain to stamp orders
- Machines for making linen cloth
- 1 tonne of hats
- 1 tonne of wool stockings

We need clothes.

And nails.

And medical supplies.

More hinges!

And TV. TV would be good ... even though it hasn't been invented yet.

- 2¼ tonnes of shoes
- An astronomer's telescope
- 4200 books, including 50 copies of *Cautions to Swearers*
- 'Toys, ribbons and other trifling articles', which were supposed to keep the Aboriginal people happy

All of this cost Britain close to £200,000. That's about £140 per person – way more money than most convicts saw in their lifetime.

Yes, they had hinges, but some important things were left behind. They set sail without the convicts' records, for example, so Phillip didn't know who had served how much of their sentence. They didn't have any spare clothes for the women convicts either. Phillip had thought of this, but then extra women were loaded at the last minute. And even though there were babies on board, they didn't have any nappies.

THE FIRST FLEET

Most convicts were English and Irish, but there were also Africans who were ex-slaves, North Americans and Frenchmen.

The ships carried:

- 568 male + 166 female = 734 convicts
- 25 convicts' wives
- 13 children of convicts
- 4 companies of marines = 212 navy soldiers
- 12 surgeons
- 28 marines' wives
- 24 marines' children
- About 400 sailors (their exact number was not counted, but they came from all over the world)

1352 rats.

And also.

And 23 ship cats.

The foxes, donkeys, goats, camels, toads and blackberries came later!

During the voyage 20 babies were born, and the oldest convict was either 82 or 62 – the records are confused. Her name was Dorothy Handland. She was sent out for the crime of lying in a court trial.

THE YOUNGEST *CONVICT*

British law said a person could not be guilty of
a crime until the grand old age of seven. There
were 34 children on the First Fleet, including John
Hudson who was sent to prison aged nine.

John was a chimney sweep – one of the worst
jobs in England. Small children
were forced to climb up inside
chimneys as narrow as
25 centimetres and clean
them out. They were
covered in sores and
injuries, as well as black
soot. They didn't wash
for years at a time.

One cold morning,
a London woman noticed
John Hudson washing
near a house. She thought that was very suspicious.
Especially as the house had been burgled a couple
of days earlier. A small, sooty footprint had been
left on a table when the thief climbed through
a broken window. More suspicious still, John had
with him a bundle of clean, adult clothes and
a pistol, all from the house.

He was arrested.

This is how his trial went:

Judge: How old are you?

John: Going on nine.

Judge: What business was you bred up in?

John: None, sometimes a chimney sweeper.

Judge: Have you any father or mother?

John: Dead.

Judge: How long ago?

John: I do not know.

And that was all John said. He didn't have a lawyer. Most criminals didn't. The judge felt sorry for John, so he only punished him for breaking into the house, not burglary.

You will be sent to Botany Bay for the rest of your life!

But I'm only *nine*!

One would wish to snatch such a boy, if one possibly could, from destruction, for he will only return to the same kind of life which he has led before.

Judge, Old Bailey, 10 December 1783

The last we know of John is that he got 50 lashes in 1791 for being outside his hut late at night. So we can't really say whether the judge's plan to give him a second chance in the new colony worked.

ARRIVAL

All 11 ships of the First Fleet got across the world in one piece. Only 30 people died on the voyage. That seems like a lot, but it was fewer than the number of people who had been dying on the hulks.

The six convict transports, three store ships and two navy ships arrived at Botany Bay between 18–20 January 1788. There was 'general joy and satisfaction'. The travellers were relieved to have made it.

Their satisfaction didn't last long, though. Botany Bay was windy, shallow and didn't have enough fresh water.

The Fleet were also amazed to find they had company from Britain's old enemy the French. On 24 January, two strange ships were spotted in the bay. They belonged to the explorer Jean-François La Pérouse.

A few convicts managed to reach the French ships and volunteered their services, hoping for a lift home. But La Pérouse turned them down 'with threats'. After that the British and French officers treated each other 'with the greatest politeness', until the French left a few weeks later.

MEETING *THE* LOCALS

The First Fleet were also surprised to find that Australia had more people living here than Cook and Banks had suggested – there were up to a million people across the continent. As the ships sailed into the bay, Aboriginal men shouted, '*Warra, warra, warra!*' In the Eora language, they were saying, 'Go away!'

The British officers didn't under-stand, although they made a fair guess. They came ashore anyway. A group of six

Eora men helpfully pointed them to fresh water. The officers gave the Eora men a mirror, some beads 'and other toys' in return.

At first, the Eora thought the sailors might be women. In 1780s England, beards weren't in fashion, but clothes were, and it was difficult to tell what was under them. An officer ordered one of his men to pull down his pants and sort out that question.

The Eora also noticed the captain had a front tooth missing, so he looked like an initiated Eora man. Except for his crazy hat, shoes, stockings and uniform, of course. So they were willing to be friendly, although cautious. They let Phillip's people land.

THE FIRST AUSTRALIA DAY

The Fleet moved on to a second place, which they called Sydney Cove. Sydney Cove was a deep harbour, much better for ships, and there was a freshwater spring. On 26 January, Phillip and his officers rowed ashore, put up the flag of Great Britain and gave three cheers.

Actually, they were too busy to officially 'take possession' of the colony until 7 February when Phillip read a proclamation. Even then they called it New South Wales, not Australia.

The Eora people, who were probably watching the show, hidden in the bush, had already named Sydney Cove *Worrong-wooree*.

Wrong name. Wrong day. That's our upside-down history for you.

THE FLEET *NEARLY FAILS*

Captain Phillip was now Governor Phillip, but the new land did not live up to British hopes. 'The fine meadows talked of in Captain Cook's voyage I could never see, though I took some pains to find them out,' grumbled one officer.

At best, the British only had tents to live in. The gum trees were hard to cut, bendy and bad for building. Only 12 convicts knew anything about carpentry anyway. Even Phillip had to wait a year and a half before he moved into a house.

Worse, the soil was bad for growing crops. The first grain harvest was a flop – it took six months to

Proclamation: an official public announcement – in this case that the land belonged to King George III and that Phillip was the Governor of the new colony.

grow but produced only two day's food. Food was all around them, of course. But the British didn't have the skills or knowledge to find it.

The marines, convicts and officers did catch some fish, but many convicts were better at stealing stores. Supplies got low and people started dying from disease caused by lack of fresh food. Nine of the ships went back to England.

By October 1788, Phillip was left with only two ships. He sent one off to Africa for emergency supplies. Everyone's rations were cut. The ship came back in May 1789, but it only had enough food for another four months.

`Famine is staring us in the face. Happy is the man that can kill a rat or a crow to make him a dainty meal.`

John Lowes, surgeon's assistant, 1790

Everyone's eyes were fixed on the horizon, waiting for ships with more supplies to rescue them.

CRASH COURSE

The British government hadn't forgotten them. They had sent a ship called the *Guardian* loaded with supplies (and more convicts) in 1789. It sailed south, to catch the Roaring Forties for a quick trip.

After it passed the Cape, the captain, Edward Riou, found that they were sailing between islands of ice. Not a good sign, you might think. You would be right. The weather turned bad and the ship hit an iceberg. It began to fill with water. Almost all those precious supplies were tossed overboard. Half the crew and the convicts abandoned ship.

Clever thinking by Riou meant that the ship stayed afloat. It sailed very slowly and soggily back to the Cape of Good Hope. Those who stayed on the ship survived, but the last of its supplies were taken off 'perfectly spoilt and useless'.

Meanwhile down-under, the First Fleet was going from bad to worse. One of their last two ships was wrecked. Rations were cut again. Per week, each person got one kilogram of very old salt pork, half a litre of dried peas and 55 grams of rice (a couple of spoonfuls).

We're all starving... So how come that black fellow's so healthy?

Imagine living on that.

'Hope is no more,' said the not-so-cheerful chief surgeon.

Finally, in June 1790, a sail came around the corner into Sydney Harbour.

But it wasn't bringing good news.

SECOND TIME LUCKY?

The new ship was carrying more than food. It was the first boat of the Second Fleet, filled with more people. Even the First Fleet was shocked by the conditions on the ships that followed.

There had been no Captain Phillip to look after this lot of convicts. The government had given the job to a company who normally transported African slaves to America.

Their heads, bodies, clothes,
blankets, were all full of
lice. They were wretched,
naked, filthy, dirty, lousy, and
many of them utterly unable
to stand, to creep, or even to
stir hand or foot.

Chaplain Richard Johnson, 1790

The company had been paid by the number of people who left England, not the number who survived.

Nearly half of the Second Fleet convicts died on the way out or after they arrived in Sydney. But fewer people meant more supplies. For all the wrong reasons, there would be enough food for everyone.

The new colony had survived.

FRENEMIES

In the Sydney language, Eora means 'here' and also 'the people' who belong 'here'. Phillip had been instructed by King George III to be friendly with 'the natives' so he gave strict orders that no one was to 'annoy' Aboriginal people or fire at them.

The Eora were actually at least seven clan groups. To start with, they kept to their daily lives and pretty much let the Fleet get on with theirs. But after a while, some of the convicts went back to their old tricks. They stole the Eora's 'spears and fizgigs, which they frequently leave in their huts when they go fishing'.

By the end of 1788, Phillip wrote that 'the natives now avoid us more than they did when we first landed'.

FRIENDSHIP BY FORCE

Convicts who kept on 'annoying' the Eora were sometimes speared, and Phillip got 'tired of this state of petty warfare'.

If they had really wanted to, the Eora might have got rid of the First Fleet early on. You may think that the Fleet's guns were more powerful than spears, but guns in the eighteenth century were slow and not very accurate. Close up, Aboriginal spears and clubs were quicker and just as deadly. The First Fleet also had limited ammunition and limited food, and they didn't know the land like the local people did.

The King's orders to Phillip were to make friends with the locals 'by every possible means'. Phillip took that literally. The next possible means he tried was kidnapping. He sent marines to a nearby bay to grab someone at random. It was a strange way to make friends. And it didn't work very well.

You'll get used to our friendly English ways.

```
To prevent his escape, a
handcuff with a rope attached
to it was fastened around
his left wrist, which at
first highly delighted him.
He called it ben-gad-ee (or
ornament). But his delight
turned to rage and hatred
when he discovered its use.
```

The capture of Arabanoo, described by
Officer Watkin Tench, December 1788

Arabanoo, the captive, was a quiet and gentle man, liked by Phillip and many others.

Occasional spearings by other Eora continued. But a more potent force than either muskets or spears was about to strike.

SCAB ESCAPE

Remember the medical supplies that were on the First Fleet? Those supplies included dried scabs in glass bottles. The infectious scabs had been collected off people who had smallpox, a disease like chickenpox but much more dangerous.

Smallpox – big effect!

Smallpox is frequently fatal, so why bring something deadly on board?

Smallpox

Because if smallpox was going around and the old scabs were inserted under the skin of a healthy person, they only got mildly sick. Gross as it seems, people were less likely to die this way. It was a bit like a vaccine.

In April 1789, smallpox got out. It spread into the Aboriginal community but not the English community (except for one sailor). Maybe the first Aboriginal people infected did have mild cases. But they passed the live disease on. The result was horrible. The Eora got very sick.

Horrified, Arabanoo tried to look after two sick children.

> Those who witnessed his expression and agony can never forget either. The rocks were filled with putrid bones of those who had fallen victim. Arabanoo lifted up his hands and eyes in silent agony for some time. At last he exclaimed, 'All dead! All dead!' and then hung his head in mournful silence.

Officer David Collins, 1789

Sadly, Arabanoo soon died from smallpox himself.

The smallpox outbreak might not have been an accident. In 1763, British troops had deliberately infected North American Indians, using blankets from the smallpox hospital. As a weapon, smallpox worked. The Aboriginal people around Sydney were almost all wiped out or ran away. And the ones who ran away took smallpox with them to other communities. We don't know how many people died across the continent. But with fewer Aboriginal people around, it was easier for the British to expand their settlement. And that's what the colonists continued to do over the next few years, going up the Parramatta River, then the Hawkesbury River in 1794.

Hawkesbury River

Parramatta River

Pt. Jackson (Sydney

Botany Bay

MORE FORCEFUL *FRIENDSHIPS*

Governor Phillip's next 'friends' were two Eora men called Bennelong and Colebee. Colebee soon escaped. But Bennelong stayed.

Bennelong was outgoing and smart. 'He willingly communicated information, sang, danced and capered, told us all the customs of his country,' said Officer Watkin Tench.

In 1790, Bennelong disappeared back to his own people. This was not what the Governor wanted. When Bennelong was seen at a feast on Manly Beach, Phillip took some soldiers out to talk him into coming back. Instead of getting Bennelong, the Governor got a spear through his shoulder. The blade went all the way through to the other side.

The marines thought he was going to die. They rowed him back to Sydney Cove. A surgeon took the spear out. Luckily for Phillip, the blade had missed his artery.

A LONG WAY FOR BENNELONG

Bennelong came to see how the Governor was and stayed. In 1792, he agreed to travel to England with Phillip when he resigned as Governor and went home.

Bennelong and another man, Yemmerrawanne, became the first Aboriginal people to travel the world. In London they were shown the sights. Bennelong learned how to smoke, skate, box and use a knife and fork. But then they both got ill. Yemmerrawanne died and Bennelong was homesick. He came back to Sydney in 1795, and became leader of an Aboriginal group of about 100 on the Parramatta River.

COMING TO TERMS WITH CHANGE

To the British, Bennelong's return to the bush proved it was impossible for Aboriginal people to learn. 'So much pains had been taken for his improvement. He has subsequently taken to the woods again and returned to his old habits,' they said. But it probably meant that Bennelong liked his old life better. 'Not me go to England no more,' he wrote to Phillip. 'I am at home now.'

Aboriginal people were learning more than the colonists realised. For example, they created words for things they had never seen before. Try to match these words from Victoria to the English words below.

ABORIGINAL WORDS

1. *Doom-doom-eburamul* Meaning 'shaped like an emu'

2. *Karl* What its growl sounds like

3. *Drumbullabul* Meaning 'thunder'

4. *Yeep* Aboriginal version of an English word

5. *Chuck-chuck* What they sound like

6. *Bullito kurun* Meaning 'big canoe'

7. *Woorooneechallup* Meaning 'mussel shell'

BAA!

ENGLISH WORDS

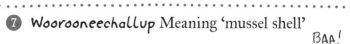

A. Farmyard birds
E. Sheep

B. Gun

C. Bottle
F. Dog

D. Ship
G. Spoon

And there were more changes ahead.

124

Joseph Banks A rich scientist who visited Down Under with Captain Cook. Recommended Botany Bay for a colony but stayed at home.

Captain Arthur Phillip In charge of the First Fleet. First Governor of New South Wales.

David Collins Phillip's deputy. He organised and judged court cases.

Surgeon General John White Head of the medical team. He looked after sick convicts from the First, Second and Third Fleets.

Watkin Tench An officer of the marines. He kept a diary and wrote two books about the colony.

Chaplain Richard Johnson The first religious minister of the colony. He was also a magistrate and successful farmer.

Arabanoo An Eora man kidnapped by Governor Phillip to get to know Aboriginal people.

Woollarawarre Bennelong A senior Eora man, also kidnapped. He was a negotiator between Europeans and Eora and one of the first two Aboriginal people to visit Europe.

Major Francis Grose Arrived in 1792 as the head of the New South Wales Corps. He filled in as Governor while the colony waited for a new one.

Bungaree A Guringai man, leader of Aboriginal people in the Sydney township. Was given the made-up title 'Chief of the Broken Bay tribe' by Governor Lachlan Macquarie. He assisted the English explorers Matthew Flinders and Phillip King on their travels.

REBELS

After four tough years as Governor, Phillip sailed home and the First Fleet marines were replaced by soldiers.

It was a major change – literally. Major Francis Grose led the new regiment, which was known as the New South Wales Corps. The colony was left in his care for a while, instead of having a Governor.

English soldiers mostly didn't want to sail down-under. So the Corps weren't the A-list. In fact, some had come out of military prisons.

The moment Phillip left, the colony changed. Grose got rid of the rule that everyone got the same rations. When food was short, Corps soldiers got more. They got more land too and had almost unlimited power.

Corps: not corpses, living army soldiers, said 'core' without the 'ps'. (The marines had been from the navy.)

Life was about to get much harder for everyone who wasn't an officer.

GROSE-LY *UNFAIR*

The Corps were above the law. If a soldier did something illegal, convicts and ex-convicts couldn't do anything about it. 'No provocation is ever to be an excuse for convicts striking a soldier,' Grose instructed in 1794. The officers of the Corps turned Sydney into a profit-making business.

The system worked like this:

- Officers took all the land from the Aboriginal people for FREE.

- Officers gave themselves the best land for FREE.

- Officers gave themselves the best convicts as workers on their land, for FREE.

- Officers took gov- ernment supplies to feed their convict workers, for FREE.

- Officers grew food supplies on their FREE land, with FREE labour.

- Officers bought all the supplies coming into Sydney on ships, with IOUs on their wages.
- Officers sold both lots of supplies back to the government stores, at VERY HIGH prices.

If you get stuff without spending money and sell it for a lot, that means fat profits.

> There were two types in the colony — those who had been transported and those who should have been.

Governor Lachlan Macquarie, 1810–1820

FUNNY MONEY

One of the things the First Fleet did not pack was actual money. Nobody thought a colony in the middle of nowhere needed coins.

In 1793, an American ship arrived in Sydney. The captain refused to sell the food he was carrying, unless the colony bought his other cargo too, which was rum, a very strong type of alcohol.

The officers got together and bought the lot, promising the ship it could collect the money in England, from their wages. After that, booze became big business. And the colony's main currency.

Currency: the system of money used.

Soldiers were paid in other goods too, like tobacco and tea. But rum gave the New South Wales Corps their nickname, the Rum Corps.

I'm sitting on my life's savings.

Eventually, in 1792, a new Governor, John Hunter, was sent to run the colony. Then Governor Philip King arrived in 1800, but the troops stayed well and truly in control.

THE CROPPIES

After 1800, Britain started sending a different kind of convict to Australia. They were Irish men, called 'croppies'. Back in Europe, the croppies had been fighting against English rule. After a failed rebellion in 1798, the English packed hundreds of Irish rebels off to New South Wales.

The English in Australia thought the Irish convicts were a 'troublesome lot'. You might think of the British as one people, but the Irish didn't. Irish convicts spoke Gaelic, not English. Their religion was Catholic instead of Protestant.

The colony's English officials were very worried that the Irish were plotting against them. Irish convicts were distrusted and mistreated. One was given 300 lashes at just the rumour of a rebellion.

Rebels: people who join a rebellion, which is an armed fight against your rulers.

> The number of Catholic
> Convicts is very great ... the
> most wild, ignorant and savage
> Race that were ever favoured
> with the light of Civilization.

Reverend Samuel Marsden, 1807

In 1804, the croppies decided they'd had enough and they would start a rebellion down-under too.

At sunset one night, led by Irish convicts Philip Cunningham and William Johnston, hundreds of croppies got together at Castle Hill, about 35 kilometres from Sydney. Around the colony, others waited for a secret signal to join them in the rebellion.

The rebels set fire to buildings and grabbed weapons and rum. They meant to take over Parramatta, then march to Sydney and hop on a few ships to go home.

LIBERTY *OR DEATH*

Some of the convicts got lost in the dark. The signal to rebel didn't get passed on. Seeing the fires, families in Parramatta panicked and escaped in boats down the Parramatta River. A messenger galloped off to Sydney to alert Governor King. Cannons were

fired and drums beaten to wake up the Rum Corps.
The soldiers marched through the night from
Sydney to Castle Hill.

The Irish rebels were fired
up with their slogan
'Liberty or death!'
They were also fired
up with a lot of
stolen rum.
But unfortunately
for them they
didn't have much
firepower – only
one gun for
every 10 men.

THE CROPPIES COP IT

The rebels and the soldiers lined up facing each
other on the slope of a hill. Major George Johnston,
who was leading the troops, dared the rebel leaders
to come forward and talk to him. Full of courage
and rum, they did. The Major and his deputy
whipped out their hidden pistols, and held them
to the rebels' heads.

The rebellion ended in death, not liberty.

CROPPIES LIE DOWN!

This was the scene as 'Major Johnston with Quartermaster Laycock and twenty five privates of ye New South Wales Corps defeats two hundred and sixty six armed rebels'. The soldier on horseback orders the croppies to lie down. The standing soldier calls them 'rebel dogs', while the Major on horseback threatens, 'I'll liberate you!' A croppy cries, 'We are all ruined!'

We don't know who drew the picture back in 1804, but you'd think it probably wasn't a croppy.

WILL THE REAL BAD GUYS PLEASE STAND UP?

It wasn't long before New South Wales went through another rebellion. But, in the upside-down way of the colony, this time the rebels weren't convicts. They were officers.

The British government had suspected for a while that the Rum Corps were giving them a rum deal. In 1806, Britain sent out a new Governor, William Bligh.

Bligh had a reputation as a mean man, but the first thing he did in New South Wales was not mean – he handed out free stores to settlers whose homes had been flooded. The Corps did not like this, because they had been selling supplies at very high prices.

The Corps disliked Bligh even more when he banned rum as money. He stopped handouts of land (except to himself and his daughter). He also kicked people out of their houses in Sydney to make way for government buildings. Landowners felt their property rights were being taken away. You might think that was a bit rich, since they had only just taken the land from the Aboriginal people, but they didn't think that way.

YOU'RE UNDER ARREST

In 1807, a convict escaped from Sydney on a ship. This ship belonged to an important officer named John Macarthur.

Macarthur liked picking fights. He had already fought two duels. He was also the paymaster for the Corps – he arranged the first rum deal and had made a pile of money since.

> Captain Macarthur was as far from honour as my nose is from silver.
>
> Joseph Holt, Irish settler, 1838

Bligh sent Macarthur an order to show up in court about the escaped convict. But Macarthur wouldn't go.

The members of the court refused to try Macarthur anyway – they were his fellow officers and mates, including Major Johnston, who had ended the 1804 croppie rebellion.

Bligh accused them all of treason. He ordered Macarthur's arrest in January 1808.

Then Johnston decided to take charge. He ordered Macarthur's release and sent the New South Wales Corps marching over to Government House.

```
Sir, you are charged of crimes
that render you unfit to
exercise supreme authority
another moment.
```

Major George Johnston's letter to
Governor William Bligh, 26 January 1808

NO! YOU'RE UNDER ARREST

The Corps aim was to arrest the Governor. At Government House, Governor Bligh's daughter defended her father with an umbrella, but the umbrella did not stop the Corps. The soldiers found Bligh in a bedroom. They said he was hiding behind the bed. He said he was hiding some documents, but nobody believed him.

Bligh had to live under house-arrest until he was put on a ship back to England the next year. In the meantime, officers of the Corps did whatever they liked, running the colony themselves. This was the only military takeover of a government in Australian history.

THE RUM REBELLION RUNS OUT

When the British government heard about the 'Rum Rebellion', they decided to recall the Corps. They sent out a new regiment of soldiers and a new Governor who was also an army officer. Macarthur and Johnston both had to go back to Britain and face court there.

This sounds like justice was done. But unlike the Irish rebels, the officers were not punished with death. They lost their jobs and kept their liberty. Both of them eventually returned to their nice big farms in Sydney to annoy the new Governor.

WHO'S IN CHARGE OF THE CONVICT COLONY? (1788-1846)

King George III (1760–1811) The ruler of Britain and therefore the colony – he didn't actually die until 1820, but in 1811 his son Prince George took over the job because the King was mentally ill.

King George IV (1820–1830) Previously in charge as Prince George, he was officially king from 1820.

King William IV (1830–1837) Another of King George III's sons.

Next in line was Queen Victoria, King George III's granddaughter, who ruled Down Under at a distance from 1837 until 1901.

They were the royals in Britain, but who was making sure everyone followed the rules down-under?

Arthur Phillip Governor of New South Wales (1788–1792)

Francis Grose Head of the New South Wales Corps; Lieutenant Governor (1792–1794)

John Hunter Governor of
New South Wales (1795–1800)

Philip King Governor of
New South Wales (1800–1806)

David Collins
First Lieutenant Governor
of Van Diemen's Land
(1804–1810)

William Bligh Governor of
New South Wales (1806–1808)

Lachlan Macquarie
Governor of New South
Wales (1810–1821)

George Johnston,
John Macarthur and the New
South Wales Corps officers
run a rebel government

Thomas Brisbane
Governor of New South
Wales (1821–1825)

Ralph Darling
Governor of New South
Wales (1825–1831)

Richard Bourke
Governor of
New South Wales
(1831–1837)

George Gipps
Governor of
New South Wales
(1838–1846)

So what was it
like under
their rule?

LAGS AND LASHES

The new Governor's job was to clean up New South Wales. By this time, the colony had 11,000 people who had spread nearly 100 kilometres inland. But Sydney's streets and buildings were as messy as its government had been. Governor Lachlan Macquarie thought they were 'in a most ruinous state'. He wanted the colony to run better and look nicer.

Macquarie picked out the most skilled convicts to work on government building projects. He employed a convict, Francis Greenway, to be his architect. Greenway had been an architect in England before he was caught faking a document and was transported. In Sydney he was allowed straightaway to set up a business designing buildings.

He probably got special treatment because his skills were so rare in the colony. So that's why Sydney's most elegant buildings and landmarks were designed by a forger and built by criminals.

SAINT MACQUARIE?

Macquarie was enthusiastic about making his mark down-under. Which of these places do you think has Macquarie's name on them?

A A park bench   C A street   F A port

B A church   D An island   G Two rivers

E A mountain

Answer: All of the above, except the park bench, which is named after his wife. Australia has a Macquarie Island, Mount Macquarie, Port Macquarie, Macquarie River, Lachlan River and Macquarie Street, and St James' Church in Sydney has his name carved on the front.

FILTHY *RICH*

In this upside-down colony there were more criminals and ex-criminals than anyone else. After they had done their time, convicts were free. And Macquarie did his best to make them respectable. He encouraged these 'emancipists' to make something of themselves. But non-convicts looked down their noses at them. 'Respectable' English people disliked the convicts having it easy.

> The punishment of transportation is nine times in ten looked upon as a summer excursion, an easy migration to a happy and better climate.
>
> Lord Ellenborough, speaking
> in the English parliament, 1810

REIBEY'S RIDES

Not all convicts did well, but some did. One famous example is the person now on our $20 note.

In 1790, 13-year-old James Burrow went for a joy ride on a horse that didn't belong to him.

Emancipists: ex-convicts who had been freed or completed their sentence.

He was arrested. At his trial, it turned out that his name didn't belong to him either.

'He' was in fact a 'she'.

Mary Reibey was given another free ride, to Sydney as a convict. She married a trader and kept his business going after he died. When Reibey returned to England for a holiday in 1820, she was so rich she became a celebrity in her home town.

Macquarie tried not to be a snob. He announced that any honest and hard-working person, 'whether Free Settler or Convict, will ever find in me a Friend and Protector'.

He invited freed convicts like Reibey to dinner. Officers and free settlers were shocked. They refused to go. 'Feelings of this kind are not easily overcome,' said the powerful English politician Lord Bathurst. He knew, because the settlers sent him and the British government long letters, complaining about Macquarie.

BIGGE *DEAL*

Macquarie was not a softie. He ordered plenty of floggings, hangings and hard labour. But Britain's rulers were nervous. In France in 1789, the poor people had risen up against the rich. Lots of lords and ladies had been killed in the French Revolution. Even the French King and Queen had been executed. The upper class in England were worried about 'the mob' running wild in Britain too.

It didn't help that Britain was tight for money, after fighting a war with France. The government was annoyed at paying for Macquarie's new buildings and improvements. They didn't want the colony to be a nice place.

> Transportation to New South Wales is intended as a severe Punishment, and must be an Object of Real Terror to all classes.

Lord Bathurst, instructions to John Bigge, 1819

Lord Bathurst sent an investigator to the colony in 1819. John Bigge spent months talking to people. He made friends with Macarthur, but not with the Governor.

Macarthur told Bigge that what New South Wales needed was a small group of rich landowners who weren't convicts. They could 'become powerful as an aristocracy'. He and his wife Elizabeth already owned land all over New South Wales so it's not hard to guess who he had in mind.

Bigge agreed with Macarthur, more or less. He wrote a very, very long report. He said convicts were getting too many 'luxurious indulgences'.

The British government decided to toughen up.

CONVICT CONDITIONS

Convicts in Australia were not slaves. They could be 'assigned' – given out as workers – to other people in the colony. They had to cut down trees, build roads, work on farms and in factories, and sometimes the conditions were very harsh. But they did have rights.

A master was not supposed to whip a convict without asking a magistrate first. If a convict behaved well, the convict could be given a 'ticket-of-leave'.

This allowed them to change jobs and move around within limits.

When their sentence was over, they would be free. They could marry, and their children would be free too.

THE CONVICT 'PAY PACKET'

Convicts only had to work for their master until three in the afternoon. After that, they were allowed to work for anyone, for pay. This wasn't as good as it sounds because employers almost always paid in food, rum or clothing and made up their own prices.

Convicts were also given a fixed ration from the government stores or from their master.

Men were supposed to get:

- **Clothes** (called 'slops') – for winter, a woollen jacket, a grey or yellow waistcoat, a pair of trousers, a pair of wool stockings, two shirts, a pair of shoes, a neckerchief and a woollen hat; for summer, the same, except an extra shirt instead of the jacket.

- **Rations** – half a kilo per day of meat, plus half to one kilo of flour, plus tea and sugar (but no fruit, vegetables or milk).

EQUAL UNDER THE LAW

In Australia's first civil-law case, convict couple Susannah and Henry Kable took a ship owner to court in 1788. The First Fleet ship they had arrived on had lost £15 worth of their belongings (worth about $4000 now). Henry Kable had been a 'businessman' who liked to do business with other people's stuff. He and his wife had both been transported for burglary, but they won the case against the ship owner for not looking after *their* belongings.

WIFE STRIFE

Not all convicts were poor people. Sir Henry Browne Hayes was transported for getting married. Sort of.

One night in 1797, he sent a fake letter to a girl called Mary – she was the rich daughter of a banker. He wanted to marry her to get his hands on her money. The letter said Mary's mother was dying. So she jumped in a coach, in the dark and the pouring rain, and raced off to see her mother.

The coach was stopped by five horsemen and Mary was kidnapped. A priest was waiting at Hayes' house to perform the marriage. Not surprisingly, Mary refused to marry him. She was locked in a room but managed to send a note to her relatives. Hayes had to go on the run.

After two years he turned himself in and was transported for being a 'bride thief'. One of Sydney's poshest suburbs – Vaucluse – is named after the mansion he built here. He was eventually pardoned and sailed back to Ireland.

CONVICT CANT

Convicts 'who crossed the herring pond' (sailed to Australia) brought their own 'cant' (slang) with them. And they invented more once they arrived.

Here's a few to stash in your noggin.

Scrubbing brush	A rough bread full of chaff that scrubbed out your insides
Sandstone	A man who crumbled easily and couldn't stand up to flogging
Canary	A convict – from his yellow uniform

Government man	A convict – employed by the government
Barking irons, bull dogs	Pistols 
Birds of a feather	Criminals in a gang 
Locksmith's daughter	A key
Captain's daughter	Cat-o'-nine-tails
Draw a wiper	Pickpocket a handkerchief
As full of money as a toad is of feathers; never a face but his own	Broke; no money in your pocket

INFAMOUS *ISLANDS*

After Bigge's report, more convicts were sent to private landowners. A bad master might work you a lot and feed you too little. But a worse fate was to be put on the iron-gangs or sent to Port Arthur in Van Diemen's Land or to Norfolk Island.

These terrible places were supposed to be for 'old lags' – difficult convicts who committed another crime after coming to Australia.

In Port Arthur men cut stone, worked naked in a coal mine and pulled carriages on a railway line. But even that was better than a new 'model' prison opened in 1850. Prisoners were locked in a sound-proof cell, with no light, for a month at a time to reflect on their misdeeds. Would that improve *your* behaviour? Many prisoners went mad.

Iron-gang: convicts who had to work chained together, often building roads.

Boys aged 9–16 were sent to Point Puer near Port Arthur. The first ones there in 1834 had to build their own dorms. Later, boys made boats, shoes, barrels and books. Those who misbehaved got the lash. For fun, they played marbles or 'Crown the Overseer' – tipping a bucket of poo over the night guard.

Women and babies might be sent to the Cascades Female Factory in Hobart. It was a damp, crowded prison. The women washed clothes, sewed and spun wool thread. They worked from dawn to sunset – more than 12 hours in summer.

If they had a baby, it was taken away to a nursery when it was only a few months old. Almost half died – at least 963 infants died in Van Diemen's Land nurseries from 1838–1858.

THE CAT'S CLAWS

The commonest punishment in the colony was to be flogged. The 'cat-o'-nine-tails' was a whip with nine cords, with knots tied along the cords. If convicts stole something, tried to escape or were rude, they got between a dozen and hundreds of lashes.

Flogging cut through your skin, sometimes down to the bone. A Norfolk Island convict described a man being 'immediately sent back to work, his back like bullock's liver and his shoes full of blood'. The only medical help he got was pig fat spread on his back with a piece of rope fluff.

WORSE *THAN DEATH*

Norfolk Island, a tiny island halfway to New Zealand, was 'a place of the extremest punishment short of Death' according to Governor Ralph Darling in 1827.

In 1834 more than 100 convicts rebelled against the guards and tried to escape. They failed. When a priest came to tell some of them they were going to be hanged, he was amazed that 'each man who heard his condemnation of death went down on his knees, and thanked God'. They were grateful 'to be delivered from this horrid place' by death.

Norfolk Island convicts were whipped, starved and worked wearing irons. 'They looked less like human beings than the shadows of gnomes,' a Sydneysider said.

> I knew a man so weak, he was thrown into the grave, when he said, 'Don't cover me up. I'm not dead ...' The overseer answered, 'Damn your eyes, you'll die tonight, and we shall have the trouble to come back again!'
>
> Joseph Smith, ex-convict, 1845

LEFT HANGING

The ultimate punishment, death by hanging, was as public as it was in Britain. One of the most horrible accounts is of the first man hanged in the South Australian colony.

Michael Magee had been sentenced to death for trying to shoot the sheriff in 1838. But the new colony didn't have convicts and it didn't have a professional hangman. The hanging was done by a man with his face masked, to keep him anonymous. He botched the job.

It took poor Michael Magee 13 minutes to die.

> ... he did not fall, and there he was hanging in the air, uttering the most excruciating cries, 'Oh God! Oh Christ! Save me!' To make it worse, he got both his hands up to the rope above his head to prevent his choking. It was a horrid sight to witness ...

Anonymous witness, Adelaide, 1838

The crowd left with 'hearts sickening and sad'.

GET LOST

It wasn't long before the colonists in New South Wales got adventurous. The land between Sydney and the Blue Mountains filled up with farms. The colonists wanted to know what was over the mountains. People tried to follow the rivers through the bush but ended up at the bottom of waterfalls and impossible cliffs.

The English explorer George Caley attempted to cross the mountains in 1804, but 'It being very slippy, and of course dangerous, I was obliged to return'. He called it 'the Devil's Wilderness'.

European explorers weren't that interested in pretty scenery. They had another purpose. They wanted to find grassland for the colony's cows and sheep.

OUT OF THE BLUE

In 1813, three British gentleman, Gregory Blaxland, William Lawson and William Wentworth, took four of their servants and several of their dogs out for a long mountain walk.

This time, they tried climbing up and along the ridges of the Blue Mountains. The men hacked through the bush and scrambled over rocks. They marked a road as they went. After three weeks, they came to the top of a mountain, from which they could see the other side.

They had beaten the Blue Mountains. Now nothing could stop 'the interior of the country from being explored, and the colony from being extended'.

AUSTRALIA'S MOST MISERABLE PLACE NAMES

Many Australian places were re-named to celebrate explorers. (Or their friends, families or rulers.) Three towns in the Blue Mountains are named after Blaxland and his mates. The English explorer Edward Eyre gave his surname to a lake in SA that had been *Kati Thanda* in the Arabana language. *Kati Tjuta* in NT became Mt Olga, after a German queen.

But these place names don't celebrate anything:

- Lake Disappointment in WA is a salt flat with no water.

- Mount Disappointment in Victoria was climbed by the explorers Hamilton Hume and William Hovell in 1824. They hoped to get a view of the sea, but too many trees got in the way.

- Mount Hopeless   we have four of these! One each in Queensland, NSW, Victoria and SA. Eyre named the one in SA because he couldn't see how to get past the salt lake at the bottom of it.

Now I can see the sea!

- Dismal Swamp is in Tasmania. In 1828 explorers found the ground there so soggy they had to sleep in trees to keep dry.

Coffin Bay in SA sounds bad but is actually named after a navy commander with an unfortunate name who helped explorer Matthew Flinders. Murdering Gully and Murdering Creek in Victoria and Queensland, however, are thought to have a nasty history.

EPIC FAILS

Explorers like Blaxland were heroes in the eyes of the colonists. But explorers also made some of the most famous fails in the history of Down Under.

One of these was the search for the inland sea. Perhaps you're thinking, What inland sea? Good point! Australia doesn't have an inland sea.

It's smaller than I expected!

The Murray and Darling Rivers flow *away* from the coast of NSW. So nineteenth-century Europeans decided there must be lots of water somewhere in the middle of the continent.

```
I feel confident we were in
the immediate vicinity of an
inland sea.
```

Explorer John Oxley's
report to the Governor, 1818

John Oxley tramped around a lot of hot and 'useless' country in NSW, carrying a boat. He didn't find the sea. Neither did Charles Sturt or Edward Eyre, in the 1820s–1840s.

'We were locked up in the desolate and heated region which we had penetrated,' Sturt said, in disappointment. He thought there had once been a sea there. He was right, but he'd arrived a few hundred thousand years too late to find it.

At least Blaxland, Lawson, Wentworth, Oxley and Sturt all came back alive. Eyre only just made it across the Nullabor Plain in 1841. His servant was killed and supplies ran out, but his guide Wylie, a Noongar man, found enough food and water to save Eyre's life. Explorers often got lost, starved or died of thirst or accident. Some were killed by Aboriginal people defending their land, or by members of their own expedition.

THE LOST EXPLORER

In 1848, a group of six European men and two
Aboriginal men led by the German explorer Ludwig
Leichhardt set out from Queensland to cross
Australia from east to west. The group had at least
seven horses, 20 mules and 50 bullocks, all loaded
up with supplies and scientific equipment.

Leichhardt had led a successful expedition
before, but somehow this one disappeared. They
were last seen 500 kilometres from Brisbane.
A search party was sent out four years later when
Leichhardt didn't arrive at his destination – a bit
late to be of any help.

Leichhardt left a trail of trees carved with the
letter L and Aboriginal stories of lost
white men. Possible
clues, including
gold coins
and an iron
tent peg,
have been
found in
north and
central
Australia.

Leichhardt's
journey of
discovery

But only one clue definitely points to Leichhardt –
a gun found inside a tree, all the way over in WA.
The gun was partly burnt, but it still had a brass
nameplate saying: *Ludwig.Leichhardt.1848*. No one
really knows how it got there.

The remains of Leichhardt and his men were
never found.

DEADLY *DISCOVERY*

In the same year, 1848, a ship dropped Edmund
Kennedy and his team off on the north coast of
Queensland. He was a surveyor – 'a fine, noble,
fellow', good at drawing, map-making and singing.
These were all useful explorer skills.

He first explored and mapped parts of
Queensland and NSW. With him on his third expe-
dition were 12 men, including an Aboriginal man,
Galmarra, from the Hunter Valley in NSW, who
Kennedy called 'Jackey Jackey'.

They aimed to explore Cape York. A ship
would drop them off and another one would pick
them up a few months later. That was the plan
anyway. Unfortunately the first ship dumped
them in a swamp. Kennedy and his men found
it almost impossible to move through the mud
and mangroves.

After two months, the party had only travelled 30 kilometres. After nearly seven months, supplies were running out and several men were sick. Kennedy decided to split the group. Kennedy, Galmarra and three others would hurry up the coast to the ship. The sick men were to wait on a beach.

Not long after, one of the five men still on the move accidentally shot himself in the shoulder. Kennedy left two men to look after him.

Kennedy and Galmarra kept going. They reached the Escape River, about 800 kilometres north of their dropping-off point. The Escape River did not live up to its name. It was swampy and swarming with crocodiles.

Kennedy's way was blocked, and the local Aboriginal people attacked. Kennedy was speared and Galmarra was wounded.

> I asked him, 'Mr Kennedy, are you going to leave me?' and he said, 'Yes, my boy. I am going to leave you.' ... I gave him paper and pencil, and he tried to write, and then he fell back and died, and I caught him as he fell back and held him, and I then turned round myself and cried.
>
> Galmarra, 1848

Galmarra was chased by their attackers but escaped on foot. He hid his tracks by wading neck-deep down a river.

He travelled 13 days alone, without supplies, until he reached the ship at the very top of Australia. Then he led rescuers to the men left waiting, although only two had survived. Galmarra was the only one of the explorers to complete the expedition.

WHERE *THERE'S A WILL*...

In 1860 the South Australian colony was sending an explorer across the continent, and Victoria wanted to beat their neighbours to it.

They chose Robert O'Hara Burke to lead their expedition. He had a reputation for getting lost – a local newspaper said 'he could not tell the north from the south in broad daylight'. But he was a policeman and ex-army officer, so the Victorian government thought he would be a good leader. Plus, they were in a bit of a hurry. A young astronomer called William Wills was made Burke's deputy.

Almost all of Melbourne turned out to cheer on the team. The stars of the show were the expedition's four Indian camel drivers and 26 camels.

The explorers were equipped with a massive 20 tonnes of luggage, including three tonnes of flour, a couple of tonnes of meat, and even coffee and chocolate. The expedition cost £57,000, more than

BARH!
BARH!

$10 million of today's money. Slowly they trundled north through Victoria, loaded down with food. 'No expedition has ever started under such favourable circumstances,' Burke said.

In western NSW, Burke decided to dump a lot of supplies. He led a few of the men into outback Queensland. At a place called Cooper Creek, which was the furthest Europeans had explored, he divided the team again, telling some of them to fetch the supplies from NSW.

All was going quite well. They were almost halfway to the north coast.

```
Everything has been very
comfortable so far; in fact,
more like a picnic party than
a serious exploration; but
I suppose we shall have some
little difficulties soon.
```

Wills' letter to his sister Bessy, 6 December 1860

THERE'S NOT ALWAYS A WAY

But then Burke got tired of waiting for the supplies. He and Wills, plus two more men, John King and Charles Gray, set out on 16 December 1860.

Burke instructed the rest of the expedition to wait three months for them. Privately, Wills suggested they should wait four months.

It took Burke, Wills, King and Gray two months to reach the north coast of Australia. They sort-of did what they set off to do – although bad weather and a mangrove swamp stopped them from even seeing the ocean.

They started running out of food on the way back. Gray died, probably of diarrhoea. When Burke, Wills and King arrived back at Cooper Creek they were so exhausted their legs felt like they were paralysed. It was four months and five days since they had left. The campsite was empty. But the men found a message scratched into a tree. It said: *DIG 3 FT. N.W. APR. 21 1861*

The rest of the expedition had left earlier on the same day. What would you have done?

A Stagger after the departed men.
B Follow the instructions on the tree.
C Light a bonfire and hope the others will see the smoke and rescue you.
D Wander off in a different direction.

Burke took option (b) to begin with. Wills and King dug a hole three feet to the north-west of the tree. They found a chest of supplies. They ate and rested. But then, instead of going after the others, Burke took option (d). He led Wills and King off into the desert, towards the nearest police station.

That seems reasonable, right? Until you know that the police station was 240 kilometres away, at a place called Mount Hopeless.

At times the three men were helped by Aboriginal people, which kept them going for a while. But heat, thirst and hunger got Burke and Wills in the end. King was the only survivor, rescued by the Yandruwandha people.

HORSE *SENSE*

Sometimes the animals did better than the humans. In 1858 McDouall Stuart, one of the most successful European explorers down-under, left a horse behind in the Nullarbor because it was lame. The sensible horse turned around and went home. It found its way back to Port Lincoln, 400 kilometres away.

Looks like dinner.

MATTHEW FLINDERS
1774–1814

Matthew Flinders was an English country boy who decided to go to sea after reading the adventure story *Robinson Crusoe*. Flinders was incredibly adventurous and incredibly unlucky. In 1795 he arrived down-under. Three years later, with his best mate George Bass, he sailed all the way around Tasmania to prove it was an island. Their boat, the *Norfolk*, was only 10 metres long.

In 1801, when he was only 26, the government gave him a bigger ship, the *Investigator*, to explore more of the coast. On board was a botanist and two artists to record what they found. The crew included a Guringai man called Bungaree.

Flinders took his beloved cat Trim on the journey too.

> Many and curious are the observations which he made, particularly in the natural history of small quadrupeds, for which he had much taste.

Matthew Flinders praising the 'scientific' work of his cat Trim, 1809

Halfway through their voyage, they discovered that the ship was rotten. But they still managed a loop around the whole of mainland Australia to show that Australia was a continent, becoming the first people (and cat) to do so.

Flinders wanted to map the coast in detail. In 1803 he set off as a passenger to England, hoping to get a replacement boat. This time he was shipwrecked, 1000km from Sydney. Flinders sailed the ship's rowboat back to Sydney and got help for the ship-wrecked crew, including Trim.

He tried again to go home, but the next ship turned out to be hopelessly leaky. Flinders got off at the island of Mauritius, near Africa. Here he struck more bad luck – Mauritius was run by the French, and England and France were at war again. The Governor of Mauritius kept Flinders under arrest for the next six years. Sadly, Trim disappeared. After Flinders was released, he finally returned to England. He died aged 40, the day after his book *A Voyage to Terra Australis* was published.

Almost everything that could go wrong did go wrong for Matthew Flinders. But he still managed to be the first person to draw a complete map of our continent and to label it 'Australia'.

NOBODY'S LAND?

From 1788, the land down-under went through one of the fastest land grabs in history. Phillip started it with 'grants' of land to marines and freed convicts for farms. In five years he gave away 1600 hectares, about the size of a large suburb. But that was nothing compared to what happened next. Grose moved things along, handing out hectares as if they were medals to the Rum Corps. Later governors were stricter about rum, but just as generous with real estate.

In 1829 the British declared that the whole of the continent was theirs, even though they had only seen a tiny part of it. By 1830, officers and some convicts had snaffled most of the good land around the areas in NSW now known as Sydney, Newcastle, Bathurst and Goulburn.

SQUATTERS

In 1834, the British government stopped free land grants. 'Waste land' could be bought from 'the Crown', which meant the British Government. In NSW, nobody was supposed to settle outside an area called the '19 Counties'.

Outside this area, the government didn't have proper maps, and they didn't have proper control, either. So plenty of people went ahead and set up farms illegally. These people were called 'squatters'. They spread far and wide, and new colonies like those in WA and SA were started.

The NSW government soon realised it was impossible to budge all the squatters. Instead, it passed a law to make squatting legal in 1836.

Squatters could stay if they paid rent of £10 a year (about $2000).

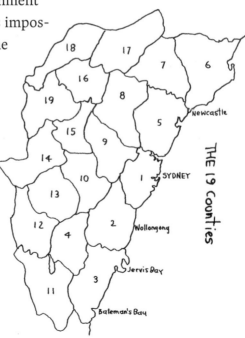

THE 19 Counties

THE STATES TAKE SHAPE

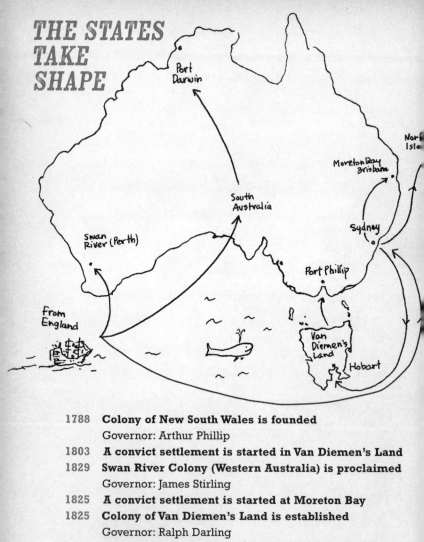

Port Darwin

Norf Isla

Moreton Bay Brisbane

South Australia

Swan River (Perth)

Sydney

Port Phillip

From England

Van Diemen's Land

Hobart

1788	**Colony of New South Wales is founded** Governor: Arthur Phillip
1803	**A convict settlement is started in Van Diemen's Land**
1829	**Swan River Colony (Western Australia) is proclaimed** Governor: James Stirling
1825	**A convict settlement is started at Moreton Bay**
1825	**Colony of Van Diemen's Land is established** Governor: Ralph Darling
1836	**South Australia is founded; it included the Northern Territory after 1863** Governor: John Hindmarsh
1851	**Port Phillip district becomes Victoria** Governor: Charles Hotham
1856	**Van Diemen's Land becomes Tasmania** Governor: Henry Fox Young
1859	**Queensland separates from New South Wales** Governor: George Bowen

BUCKLEY'S CHANCE

In 1803, William Buckley was one of the convicts who arrived from England to start a British settlement close to where Melbourne is now. One night he escaped. The English soldiers gave up on finding him – they figured he wouldn't survive in the bush. That's where we get the phrase 'Buckley's chance', meaning no chance at all.

For a few months Buckley lived by himself, eating shellfish and berries. He got tired of living alone, but the British had packed up and gone.

Buckley began to get weaker. So when he found a spear stuck in a mound grave, he took it as a walking stick. He walked a bit further and then collapsed. A group of Wathaurung people found him. Because he was carrying the spear, they thought he was the buried warrior come back from the dead.

Buckley lived with the Wathaurung people, on and off, for 32 years. With their help, it turned out he had a very good chance.

> How easy it is for the human
> being, to change his habits,
> taste, and I may add, feelings.
>
> William Buckley, 1852

In 1835 the big sailing ships came back, along with a group of settlers led by John Batman. The very tall Buckley walked into their camp, dressed in kangaroo skins. He caused 'great surprise and no small alarm'.

Buckley began to remember bits of English. The British men worked out who he was. He was offered a pardon and the generous salary of £50 a year. His job was to help explore what is now Victoria and to speak to Aboriginal people for the colonists.

DEAL *OR NO* DEAL?

Batman presented a 'treaty' to Wurundjeri elders to rent the land that is now Melbourne.

He agreed to give the 'chiefs' 20 pairs of blankets, 30 tomahawks, 100 knives, 50 pairs of scissors, 30 looking glasses, 200 handkerchiefs, 100 pounds of flour and six shirts for their land.

Would you give away your family home for that? It doesn't sound like a fair deal, does it? But at the time, Buckley was the only person who could see

Treaty: a contract between states or rulers.

what was happening
from both sides.

He was not
impressed. He knew the
Wurundjeri people didn't
have 'chiefs' who could
buy and sell the land.
That wasn't how their
society worked. And he
knew the soil was worth
more to the Europeans
than they paid.

John Batman tries to buy
tribal lands for a cartload of
stuff he got at the $2 shop.

175

```
I looked upon the land dealing
as another hoax of the white
man.
```

William Buckley, 1852

NO *DEAL*

When Governor Richard Bourke of NSW heard
about Batman's treaty he wasn't impressed either.
Not because the Wurundjeri people had got a bad
deal. No, it was because the British considered that
the land down-under was 'vacant'. Therefore it now
belonged to King William IV.

Bourke thought that neither Batman nor the

Vacant: a place with nobody in it. That meant
Australia was 'terra nullius', nobody's land.

Aboriginal people had the right to make a deal. Only the British government could decide who got what.

> All Persons without the license or authority of His Majesty's Government will be considered as trespassers upon the vacant Lands of the Crown.
>
> Governor Richard Bourke, 26 August 1835

From this point onwards, the Aboriginal people of Australia were officially trespassing on their own land.

Buckley kept sticking up for Aboriginal people. He said 'that he should rejoice if the whites could be driven away so that the aborigines could have the country to themselves again'. But in 1837 he gave up. Or

WILLIAM
BUCKLEY

perhaps he was forced to give up. He moved (or was removed) to Tasmania.

Aboriginal Australians had much worse than Buckley's chance. The British colonies would threaten their very survival.

THE WAR
THAT WASN'T

At first, some Aboriginal people thought white people were dead relatives come back to life. They wanted to treat them like family. But most Europeans didn't want to be family – they didn't think Aboriginal people were their equals. The more Europeans spread out across Australia, the more conflict there was.

Squatters took over the waterholes and cut down trees. Sheep ate the best plants. Aboriginal families lost their food, their land and often their lives. Shepherds thought 'as little of firing at a black, as at a bird', the explorer Eyre said. They also kidnapped Aboriginal women for wives, and children as servants.

THE *BLACK* LINE

By the 1820s the colonists and the Aboriginal people were raiding and killing each other in Van Diemen's Land. In 1828 Governor George Arthur divided the island into two parts on a map. Any Aboriginal person who came into the 'settled' districts could be shot.

In 1830 he tried again to 'solve' the problem – 2000 settlers and convicts marched across the island to trap the Aboriginal people on the Tasman Peninsula. The 'Black Line' cost £30,000 (millions in today's money) and took seven weeks. But only two Aboriginal men were captured and three were killed.

The Governor's final solution was to talk, trick and force all remaining Aboriginal Tasmanians onto Flinders Island. Only 43 people survived the next decade of bad diet and disease (see page 189 for how they managed to get home again).

In about 1828, the Governor put out this poster to warn everyone to behave. It looks fair. But could everyone have lived peacefully under English law? That's not how it happened anyway. An uncounted number of Aboriginal people, probably hundreds, were killed. But no colonists were hanged for the killing of Tasmanian Aboriginal people.

A BAD DOSE OF DOUGH

Some colonists thought that they could improve Aboriginal people's lives by making them more European. Well-meant gifts were sometimes taken the wrong way.

A Larumbanda man described how strange people turned up in western Queensland.

> My father had just speared a stingray when he heard the people calling out, 'Look out, everybody, the ships of the men with faces of white pipe-clay are coming again!'

Dick Roughsey, Mornington Island

The 'white pipe-clay' men left gifts behind on the beach. The Larumbanda people thought the flour was white ochre and used it to paint their bodies. The bars of soap 'seemed better tucker', they thought. So the women put them in the fire to soften and 'cook'. When the children ate the soap, they got terrible stomach pains. The adults thought the 'food' had been poisoned.

They had good reason to be suspicious. In 1839, settlers in Victoria handed out flour to the Daung Wurrung people, to make 'sweet damper'. It didn't have sugar in it, though. The flour was

spiked with the poison arsenic, in deadly doses.

'A WAR OF EXTERMINATION'

When Aboriginal people struck back, it became all-out war – a NSW magistrate in 1838 called it a 'war of extermination' to wipe out Aboriginal people.

Britain never officially declared war, unlike in New Zealand against the Māori, but many saw it that way.

```
We are invading their country.
They look upon us as enemies
and we must do the same by
them. Shoot those you cannot
get at and hang those that you
do catch on the nearest tree
as an example to the rest.
```

Northern Territory Times newspaper, 25 October 1875

CREEPY CREEKS

Myall Creek in NSW is one of the most famous scenes of this war. The details of the story are too horrible to tell here. In 1838, 28 Wirrayaraay people, including women and babies, were slaughtered with swords.

The Myall Creek massacre is not famous because it was the worst or because it was unusual. There were more than 150 known massacres of Aboriginal people in eastern Australia in the century after 1788.

At Warrigal Creek in Victoria, as many as 170 people were killed in revenge for the death of one squatter. That death was revenge for the killing of Aboriginal people. You can see who lost the most lives.

Myall Creek is famous because white convicts and ex-convicts were actually charged with murder. Sydney society was shocked – not by the murders, but by the charges. Three settlers reported the crime and gave detailed evidence in court, and Governor George Gipps made sure the crime was investigated. But even then the men got off on the first trial.

> I knew well they were guilty of murder ... but I for one would never see a white man suffer for shooting a black.
>
> Jury member, 1838

After a second trial on new charges, seven men were found guilty and hanged. They were the first British citizens executed for killing Aboriginal people.

POLICE *PROTECTION?*

'Native Police Forces' were started by colony governments in the 1840s. Aboriginal policemen were good at tracking. The promise of a horse, a gun and a pay packet – things usually restricted to Europeans – could have convinced some men to sign up. Mostly they were recruited far from where they would be working and were led by a British officer.

In Queensland especially, from 1848 to 1905, the police did the opposite of protecting. It was their job to 'disperse' any large gathering of Aboriginal people. 'Disperse' usually means to break up and spread out, but here it meant 'shoot'. In 1861 a government minister told parliament that dispersing 'meant nothing but firing at them'.

HELP O R HURT

The Governor of NSW appointed a 'Chief Protector of Aborigines' in 1839. His job was to protect the lives of Aboriginal people by 'civilising' them.

He provided blankets and clothes and education. But most Aboriginal people did not choose to be 'civilised' the way he wanted. Nor could he stop the violence between them and the settlers.

So in 1848 the British government ordered its colonies to set up 'reserves'. These were little pieces of land where Aboriginal people went to live, whether they wanted to or not. The government argued it was all right to move Aboriginal people around without giving them a choice.

> The black should, when necessary, be coerced, just as we coerce children and lunatics who cannot take care of themselves.
>
> Edward Curr,
> Board for the Protection of Aborigines, 1877

'Coerce' usually means 'force'. But here the government claimed it meant 'look after'. Who needs enemies when you have 'protectors' like that?

MOST WANTED WARRIORS

Aboriginal people across the country fought back. Most rebel groups were not led by one person, but there were some memorable fighters.

PEMULWUY

Pemulwuy was a Bidjigal man respected by Eora people as a leader and a sorcerer. To the Governor he was 'a terrible pest' but also 'a brave and independent character'. In 1790, he killed a convict. Then from 1792 he led raids against farms, stealing crops and burning houses.

This one hurt a bit!

In one battle Pemulwuy survived seven bullets. He was caught, then later escaped even though he was wearing a leg-iron. But he was eventually killed in 1802.

TARENORERER

Tarenorerer was a Tommeginne woman who led Tasmanian men and women against settlers in the early days of Van Diemen's Land. In her teens she had been kidnapped and sold to white sealers. She learned English and how to use guns, and in 1828 she returned to her country in Tasmania.

Tarenorerer trained her people to use muskets

and taught them how to wait until their enemy was reloading before attacking.

The Chief Protector of Aborigines said that she and her people had done 'nearly all the mischief upon the different settlements'. But she was captured, and she died of flu in 1831.

WINDRADYNE

When Governor Macquarie first travelled beyond the Blue Mountains in NSW, one of his officers thought the Wiradjuri locals 'were perfectly mild and cheerful'. The Wiradjuri mood changed when settlers took over their land and sacred places and shot their families. In return, from 1822, Windradyne and other Wiradjuri men speared cattle and killed shepherds.

Windradyne was a strong, 'noble' looking warrior. A Sydney newspaper reported that when he was first caught, it 'took six men to secure him and they had actually to break a musket over his body before he yielded'. Windradyne spent a month in gaol, then he went back to his 'outrages'.

Extra soldiers were sent over the mountains to deal with the Wiradjuri warriors. When the warriors disappeared into the bush, the soldiers began shooting large numbers of women and children. Many Wiradjuri men then surrendered.

Windradyne led the Wiradjuri, months later, to the Governor's yearly feast for Aboriginal communities. He was wearing a hat with 'peace' written on it. It was a clever move – the Governor had to give him a pardon.

YAGAN

Yagan was a Noongar man who was in his early thirties in 1829 when the British first came to the Perth area. It wasn't long before there was conflict.

Yagan and his father killed a settler, as payback for the killing of a Noongar boy. After more violence on both sides, Yagan was outlawed and his father was executed without a proper trial.

A reward was offered for Yagan, dead or alive. A farmer advised him not to revenge his father's death. But Yagan 'scowled a look of daring defiance, and turned on his heel'.

Not long after, Yagan was shot dead by a teenage stockman for the reward.

JANDAMARRA

Jandamarra was a young Bunuba stockman in the Kimberley region of WA. He was a skilled horseman, and when his station manager, Bill Richardson, joined the police, Jandamarra helped him track and remove Aboriginal people.

They made a crack team until betraying his people got too much for Jandamarra. When

Richardson rounded up Bunuba elders in 1894, Jandamarra shot him. Jandamarra trained and led his people in daring attacks, trying to stop stations from taking over more Bunuba country.

Helped by the Bunuba community, Jandamarra lived on the run for three years, seeming to disappear into the rocky cliffs. But he was tracked down and shot in 1897.

WAR WITH WORDS

Not all Aboriginal people fought with spears and guns. Some of them used British law and English words instead. The Tasmanians forced onto Flinders Island wrote a petition to Queen Victoria. They told her that, although they were her 'free children', the British Superintendent was treating them badly. The petition got them into even more trouble so one woman, Mary Ann Arthur, wrote to the Governor.

```
I thank my Father the Governor
that he has told us black people
that we might write him ... The
Superintendent talks plenty
about putting us into jail and
that he will hang us for helping
to write the petition to the
Queen from our country people.
We do not like to be his slaves
nor wish our poor Country to be
treated badly.
```

Mary Ann Arthur, 1846

The petition worked. In 1847 the Governor allowed Arthur's people to go back to Hobart.

A BLOCK OF MY LAND, PLEASE

In Victoria a young Wurundjeri man called Simon Wonga teamed up with a Scottish Reverend, John Green. They managed to get some land from the government for Wonga's people to 'sit down, plant corn, potatoes, and work like [a] white man'.

But by the 1870s the government had changed its mind. It planned to take back the Corranderk Reserve. Wonga's cousin William Barak wrote letters of protest and led visits to politicians. The Board for the Protection of Aborigines was so sure that Aboriginal people weren't smart enough to write the letters that they asked a detective to check the handwriting!

Barak walked to Melbourne and got a parliamentary enquiry to listen to the people of Corranderk. But in 1886 the parliament introduced a sneaky law called the 'Half-Caste Act'. It meant the government could make young people leave the reserve if it didn't think the person's skin was dark enough. Families were broken up, and the land lost its workers.

Corranderk and the other reserves were given away bit by bit to European landowners.

However the first Australians fought, with words or weapons, they were knocked down but not out.

AUSTRALIA'S MOST WANTED

The colonies had other fighters to deal with too. Some convicts didn't wait around to be flogged or hanged. They 'bolted' into the bush, where they often turned back to crime.

> They are desperate men; steeped to the very lips in crime of the deepest dye. No half-measures should be taken; it must be 'war to the knife,' and instant capture or annihilation.
>
> *Colonial Times* newspaper, Hobart, 5 April 1842

Here are some of Australia's most outrageous outlaws.

THE BLOODY DIARY BUSHRANGER

Michael Howe led a gang of up to 28 men ranging across Van Diemen's Land between 1814 and 1818. He made a diary of kangaroo skin. He wrote his nightmares in it, using blood. With the same ink, Howe also wrote an angry letter to Lieutenant-Governor Thomas Davey.

> We think ourselves Greatly
> Injured by the Country at
> Large. We are as much
> Inclined to take Life
> as you are in your hearts.
>
> Michael Howe, 1816

FEMALE BUSHRANGERS

No colonial woman ran her own gang. But we know of two women who lived on the run. Both of them were called Mary.

'Black Mary' was an Aboriginal woman

Keep me covered, Georgia!

kidnapped by Howe. After he left Mary behind in 1817, she tracked him down and betrayed him.

Mary Ann Bugg was the daughter of a British convict and an Aboriginal woman. She kept Fred Ward, known as Captain Thunderbolt, company during the 1860s. She dressed as a man, acted as Ward's scout and looked after their camp in the NSW bush until they separated.

THE CHEEKIEST BUSHRANGER

Matthew Brady was a handsome young convict who escaped from Sarah Island, a prison island in Van Diemen's Land, in 1824. He led a gang of up to 100 men.

Governor Arthur offered a reward of £25 for the capture of any member of the gang. In reply, Brady cheekily stuck up his own notice on the door of a pub. He offered 20 gallons of rum to anyone who would bring Arthur to *him*.

Scout: someone who looks out for danger or opportunities – there were no badges in the bush then!

Brady was well-liked, but the Governor got him in the end.

A bushranger's life is
wretched and miserable. There
is constant fear of capture
and the least noise in the
bush is startling. There is
no peace, day and night.

Matthew Brady, 1826

A CANNIBAL BUSHRANGER

Alexander Pearce escaped from Sarah Island in 1822 with seven other convicts. He was caught several months later, alone.

In gaol he admitted that he had eaten five of the other men. When it got down to the last two of them, neither dared to sleep for several nights. Pearce obviously stayed awake the longest.

The magistrate didn't believe Pearce. He was sent back to the island where he escaped again, with one young convict. He was recaptured and brought back alone again. This time he had pieces of the other escapee in his pocket. 'Human flesh was by far preferable' to fish or pork, he said. He was hanged.

THE CELEBRITY BUSHRANGER

Bold Jack Donahoe was an Irish convict and bushranger, who had a popular song made up about him. He died in a shoot-out in 1830. A Sydney shopkeeper sold souvenir pipes – the bowl of the pipe looked like Donahoe's head, complete with bullet-hole.

The song survived much longer than the bushranger. People still sing a version of it called 'The Wild Colonial Boy'.

```
So come along my hearties
And we'll roam the
   mountains high
Together we will plunder
And together we will die.
```

The Wild Colonial Boy, Anonymous, 1800s

The Scene of Ben Hall's Capture and Death near Forbes, New South Wales.

FIRE POWER

Troopers, settlers and bushrangers all used 'black powder' weapons. Before every shot, their guns had to be loaded with gunpowder down the muzzle. This could take minutes. After every few shots the barrel had to be cleaned. Gun battles were quite slow and very smoky (as you can see in the 1865 picture above).

Black powder weapons could be very dangerous to the user. If the weather was wet, the gun might not go off at all. Or a stray spark might make the powder go off when you weren't ready. In 1839 a customer in Melbourne's first gun store carelessly let his gun go off into a powder box. The shop and everyone in it blew up in a ball of fire.

A *STICK-UP*

A mail coach carrying a load of gold was a rolling target. 'Stick-ups' were roadside robberies by bushrangers with guns.

In an instant, six men dressed in red serge shirts and red nightcaps, with faces blacked, showed themselves from behind a rock. At the word 'Fire,' they delivered their bullets. No sooner had the six bushrangers delivered their fire than they fell back and were replaced by five or six others. The horses ran in among a lot of broken rocks, upsetting the coach. Seeing the coach capsized, the bushrangers began to cheer and rushed down pell-mell to secure their booty.

Empire newspaper, 24 June 1862

This image shows the capture and death of the bushranger Ben Hall who took part in the stick-up described above. In 1865 the government passed a law allowing anyone to kill him on sight.

BIGGEST **BUSHRANGER HAUL**

In 1854, the Bank of Victoria in Ballarat was held up by four men, with unloaded pistols. Notes and gold worth £18,000 were stolen – a couple of million in today's money.

The men got away with their loot and celebrated at the pub. But the banker had recorded the numbers from the stolen banknotes.

The landlady of the hotel stole some of the loot from the bushrangers. When she tried to spend a £20 note, it was recognised. The four bushrangers were all arrested.

MOST ESCAPED **BUSHRANGER**

William Westwood escaped at least six times in 10 years – first from his nasty employer, then from an iron-gang, then from a lock-up near Sydney, even though he was in chains. When he was recaptured and sent to Port Arthur, he escaped three times, once by swimming. Other convicts who tried to escape with him were eaten by sharks.

Westwood was known as a 'gentleman bushranger', but he was finally sent to Norfolk Island, and his only escape was death.

The cool intrepidity
and daring of this man
is astonishing. He is
well-dressed, assumes
all disguises ...
instead of the expected
gentleman you find a
highwayman,
with a brace of pistols
levelled at your breast.

The Australian newspaper, 1841

MOST VICIOUS BUSHRANGER

A couple of outlaws were in the running for this title. Many bushrangers were brutal men. Mad Dog Morgan killed several policemen in the 1860s. He was going to kill a station manager too, until the man's wife stood in front of him and begged him not to. Morgan agreed. Instead, the manager had to hold up one hand, which was shot off. Morgan allowed a young stockman to go get a doctor. But then he changed his mind and shot the stockman dead.

However the prize should go to Thomas Jeffries. On the run in 1825, he held a mother and child hostage. The mother was walking too slowly for Jeffries' liking so he killed her five-month-old baby.

His other crimes were just as terrible. Jeffries was eventually hanged at the same time as Matthew Brady (the Cheekiest Bushranger), who was disgusted that he had to die next to such an awful man.

THE ARMOURED BUSHRANGER

The infamous Ned Kelly and his gang were the only Australian bushrangers to wear armour. Kelly got a blacksmith to make the armour and helmet out of farm equipment. It was very heavy. Kelly was a big Irish bloke, and strong enough to carry its 41.4 kilo-gram weight.

Kelly hated the police and the English, who he felt were oppressing the Irish people in Australia. He wrote a long and fiery letter defending himself. He was quicker to use bullets and insults than full stops or commas.

```
A parcel of big ugly fat-
necked wombat headed big
bellied magpie legged narrow
hipped splaw-footed sons of
Irish Bailiffs or engzlish
landlords which is better
known as Officers of Justice
or Victorian Police
```

Ned Kelly, the Jerilderie letter, 1879

Kelly threatened anyone who helped the police. He said he would peg them on an ant-bed and pour fat 'down their throat boiling hot'.

Finally Kelly came to a violent end. His armour helped him survive a shoot-out, but it didn't cover his legs, and that's how he was brought down. He recovered from his bullet wounds, but was hanged in 1880. A newspaper reported that his last words were: 'Such is life.'

KEEPING A HEAD OF CRIME

The governors and the police had some gruesome ways of dealing with Australia's most wanted. They put bushranger's bodies on public display and made plaster casts of their heads after death. They even cut off the heads of slain Aboriginal warriors. Pemulwuy's head was bottled in alcohol and sent to Joseph Banks in England. Yagan was treated in much the same way. And Jandamarra's head was sent to Britain, to the manufacturer of the gun that killed him.

HOW AUSTRALIA GOT STINKING RICH

The first thing ever sold to the world from Down Under (not counting sea cucumbers) was not something you'd expect. It wasn't iron or coal or any of the things Australia sells today. It came from whales.

Governor Phillip's first job as a boy had been on a whaling ship. When he came to Botany Bay he noticed how many whales there were. In those days you didn't have to go out on a tour to spot one. Families of whales came cruising into Sydney Harbour, and even washed up on the beaches. Hobart's river had so many whales the ships almost ran into them.

This was good news for the British.

NEW SOUTH WHALES

Phillip wrote home about the whales, and the Third Fleet, which arrived in 1791, included five whaling boats. They went home loaded up with cargo.

HOW TO USE A WHOLE WHALE

What did people want whales for?

In the days before plastic and petrol, whales were a swimming supermarket of useful stuff. You won't find any weird whale bits in your local store any more, but in the 1880s whales were very handy.

- **Whalebone** was made into knives and forks and other utensils.
- **Baleen** – the bony plate in the mouth of krill-eating whales – was used for umbrellas, corsets and hoops.
- **Ambergris** – lumps of cholesterol from a sperm whale's gut – went into perfume and ointments.
- **Spermaceti oil** was drained from the head of a deep sea whale and used for make-up.
- **Blubber** was boiled down into oil, used for soap, candles, engine grease and cooking.

- **Whale meat** was eaten – it tastes like fishy beef.
- **Whalebone** could also be carved into art called scrimshaw.

SMELLY *BUSINESS*

By 1836, 39 whaling ships worked from Sydney. Just one sperm whale could provide 13,000 litres of oil. That was worth over £1000 (about 30 years' wages) in London. Whaling down-under became so sucessful that it nearly wiped out several species of whale.

The whalers made a lot of money but also a terrible pong. The smell of rotting whales and boiling blubber was so bad that the whalers had to move their business away from town.

Mosman, across the harbour from Sydney Cove, is now one of the most expensive parts of Sydney. In the nineteenth century it was the stinkiest.

You may think whales are gentle giants who only chomp on little krill. Not always. This picture from 1877 is called 'Perilous position of a whaling crew – the whale seizes the boat in its huge jaw'. Before harpoon guns and steamboats were used in the 1890s, whaling was a very dangerous job. Sometimes the whale won, and it was the whalers who lost their lives.

HOW TO KILL A WHALE

Some whaling ships went far out to sea looking for whales. When they spotted their prey, the men lowered rowboats from the main ship. They rowed close enough to spear the whale with a harpoon. The whales put up a huge fight. They thrashed their tails and even 'chawed' the boat. The harpoon was attached to the rowboat by a rope.

A dying whale would try to escape and could tow the rowboat for hours or even days. Once the whale was dead, it was hauled onto the ship or the shore and chopped up.

Chawed: an old-fashioned way of saying 'chewed'.

A KILLER COMBINATION

On the NSW coast at Eden, colonial whalers took
over from the Yuin people who had cooperated with
a type of dolphin – called an orca or a killer whale –
to bring whales to shore.

The orcas found a whale and herded it into the
bay. Then they got the attention of the whalers by
breaching and whacking the water with their tails
and rushing back and forth 'like enthusiastic dogs'.
The orcas knew which whaling boats were the
friendliest, and the whalers gave each orca a name.

When the whale had been harpooned and killed,
it sank. The orcas then ate their favourite bit – its
tongue and lips. A day or two later, the rest of the
whale body floated to the surface. The whalers
came and got it. This partnership went on until
later whalers got greedy and hunted the orcas too.

SEAL **YOUR** FATE

The colonists also found seals around Australia. Seals were almost as useful (and smelly) as whales. They have blubber, and fur seals have beautiful skins. Unfortunately for the seals, they are easier to hunt than whales – they like to lie around on rocks all day.

In the 1800s, from the age of 10 you could sign up for the bloody job of killing seals. And if you were a Tasmanian Aboriginal woman or child, you might be kidnapped and forced to take the job (just like Tarenorerer from page 186).

Being a sealer was not a nice fate. They were abandoned for months on a rocky island with only seal-meat for food, and only came home when they had shot or clubbed a shipload of seals. Sealers worked hard – so hard they worked themselves out of a job. In 1804 alone, 107,000 seals were killed. After a few years, the seals were all dead and the sealers had to go further away to South Australia.

FURRY **FOREIGNERS**

In other parts of Australia, another sort of animal was making money for the colony. The Rum Corps officer John Macarthur brought Spanish sheep called 'merinos' to NSW. His wife did a good job of looking after them while he was busy with duels, rebellions and trials.

The merinos grew nice, fine wool. In 1827, a bale of Macarthur wool sold for the record price of 196 pence per pound of wool (864 cents per kilogram). That record wasn't broken for more than a century.

Merino wool made the Macarthurs wealthy. And it gave all the upper-class, non-convict colonists a nickname – they were called 'pure merinos'.

The squatters got woolly ideas too.

> Most gentlemen have their whole souls felted up in wools, fleeces, flocks and stock. I have often sat through a weary dinner without hearing a single syllable on any other subject.

Louisa Meredith,
Notes and Sketches of NSW, 1844

The more land the squatters and pure merinos took over, the more wool they sold. By 1834, NSW sold about 800,000 kilograms of wool a year (enough for a million jumpers). Wool became Australia's top earner. But the land down-under suffered under the flocks' feet. The long grass was eaten and trampled. The soil was bare. The ground cracked.

```
Ruts seven, eight and ten feet
deep, and as wide, are found
for miles, where two years ago
it was covered with tussocky
grass. The lands here are
getting of less value every
day.
```

John Robertson, Victorian squatter, 1853

UNDERCOVER *INVADERS*

As Europeans settled in, they wanted Australia to look like 'home'.

An 'Acclimatisation Society' was started in Melbourne in 1861. It encouraged people to bring foreign plants and animals to Australia. The Governor of Victoria wanted 'all the delicacies of London and Paris' to reach his plate. Others just thought it would be fun.

Acclimatisation: usually means changing to suit the environment. To the colonists it meant changing the environment to suit themselves.

> I am for the acclimatisation
> of monkeys because they are
> exceedingly amusing.

Edward Wilson, founder of
the Acclimatisation Society, 1862

Rabbits were brought down-under by the First
Fleet for food. Wild rabbits and foxes were let go on
purpose in the 1850s for English gentlemen to hunt.
The foxes were better hunters than the men. And
the rabbits gobbled grass and turned paddocks into
a minefield of underground holes.

The settlers didn't stop at rabbits and foxes.
Which of these animals found wild in Australia are
invaders and which belong here?

- Deer
- Camels
- Cockroaches
- Horses
- Pigs
- Cats
- Goats
- Mice
- Rats

- Blackbirds
- Sparrows

- Starlings
- Water Buffalo

What harm can a few cuddly animals do?

Tweet!

Answer: Only some types of rats, mice and cockroaches are native to Australia.

Ships' crews often kept cats to catch rats and mice – like Flinders' cat Trim from page 168. In the late 1800s, cats were released into the wild to control the rabbits. However cats can be picky eaters. Inconveniently, they preferred bilbies, native birds and even grasshoppers. Modern scientists have found wild cats with 30–40 lizards and frogs in their stomach at one time.

Some introduced animals spread diseases. Cane toads are poisonous to animals that try to eat them. The native animals struggled to compete for food. And then there were the weeds. Plants like willows and blackberry choked out native plants.

LE **KANGOUROU**

Acclimatisation was a fad in France too. The French Society offered a prize to anyone able to breed kangaroos in Europe.

There have been no sightings of roos hopping past the Eiffel Tower or sipping from the Seine River so we can assume the attempt wasn't successful.

Skippy in Paris

EVEN MORE
BOAT PEOPLE

For the colony to make lots more money, it needed more workers – workers who knew how to make and grow stuff, not just steal it. So from the 1830s, the British government paid ship owners to bring people from Britain who weren't convicts. Those who came by choice were called free settlers, emigrants or 'Jemmy Grants'.

Then after the 1840s, waves of people landed on Australia's shores. They came from far away in Europe and from Australia's neighbourhood. Many were desperate for a better life. Some never wanted to leave home in the first place.

It started with mouldy potatoes ...

ROTTEN *POTATOES*

Ireland and Scotland are both green and rainy places. Ireland had lots of food. It sold butter, meat and wheat to England. But 3 million Irish people were too poor to buy any of that. They could only afford potatoes.

In 1844, a new type of mould arrived in Europe, probably on the supplies of ships from America. Unfortunately for the Irish, the mould liked their type of potato. It spread everywhere. Potato plants rotted in the fields, and the Irish people began to starve.

In Scotland, rich landlords decided they didn't want crops on their land any more. They preferred sheep. They didn't want the poor farmers either. So they pulled down the farmers' homes and made them leave. Australia and America were once again good places to get rid of Britain's unwanted people.

Emigration is the removal
of a diseased and damaged part
of our population.
It is a relief to the rest
of the population to be rid
of this part.

The Scotsman newspaper, 1851

ALL AT SEA

Sailing ships were much smaller than modern ships yet hundreds of passengers were crammed on.

Rich passengers paid for a cabin of their own. Everyone else was packed below decks, in the space called 'steerage'. Young men were kept separate from young women, but all the families were jumbled together. Children didn't count, so they shared a bunk or hammock with their parents.

The bunks were like wooden shelves, with boards between the passengers to stop them rolling on each other. Steerage was like a cross between a crate and a floating camp dormitory, but with your parents and strangers and terrible food.

Sleeping on boards with terrible food... lice, fleas and fighting off the rats. I'm only rating this *one* star on UK B&B!

$SHIP$-**SHAPE**

A sailing ship was a topsy-turvy world, especially
in a storm. Wind and waves could tip the ship
sideways. Passengers hung on for dear life. Often
people, food and luggage were tipped together onto
the floor.

```
The floor was strewed with
biscuits - flour - suet -
oatmeal - rice - meat - butter
- baskets - tinware etc etc.
And sometimes we were rolling
amongst them. Some were
laughing and some were crying
out with fear.
```

Joseph Tarry, a traveller, 1853

What were the toilets like? Men went straight
into the sea. They were supposed to use the down-
wind side of the ship for this, so that everything
blew away from the deck and other people.

Women and children used a 'water closet' below
decks. This was basically a bucket in a cupboard.
The buckets sometimes spilled in storms and
the only way to clean up was to slosh more
seawater around.

If you got wet there was no dryer for you or your clothes or your mattress. All clothes, including nappies, were washed in seawater. Salt water makes cloth stiff and scratchy. The poor babies must have had very itchy bottoms.

SECRET STOWAWAYS

These conditions were not very safe or hygienic. Some passengers never made it down-under. Lots of people got sick and many died.

Nasty illnesses like smallpox and tuberculosis spread from one person to the next. A single barrel of bad water could give the whole ship typhoid or cholera. One lousy little louse might carry typhus, which it would then deposit all over the place in its droppings. On the worst ships, up to a third of the passengers and crew died.

Ha, ha, tricked them I'm not dead.

Soon will be!

Typhoid, cholera and typhus are said 'tie-foid', 'col-u-ra' and 'tie-fus', although their names mattered less than their fatal effects.

DIARY *OF* DEATHS

Not every ship carried fatal diseases. But the food on board could be so bad that children couldn't eat it.

In 1852, a father sailed down-under with his wife and four kids. George was 14, Henry was 12, Charles, six, and Susan, four. On the voyage 50 of the 482 people on-board died, including 13 newborn babies. The father watched two of his children get sick and pass away.

12th January

Fine day not so hot. Henry & Susan still very poorly. They are dwindling. One child died this morning.

19th January

Fine day. Another child died today from starvation. A perfect skeleton.

6th March

About 9 o'clock my dear little girl breathed her last. A dead calm. At 1/2 past 10 PM they committed my child to the Deep.

Diary of Henry Knight, 1852

SHIPWRECK

A storm at sea could do worse than spill your dinner. It could sink your whole ship.

There were fewer shipwrecks than you might think – no convict ships went down in the first 45 years of the colony. That says a lot for the skill of the sailors. However, nobody knew in advance whether their ship was going to make it or be the first one to sink.

That finally happened in 1833. A ship called the *Amphitrite* – loaded with more than a hundred convict women and children – didn't get very far in its journey down-under. They hit a sandbar near a French town. The officer in charge wouldn't allow the convicts off the ship. He thought they might escape. Instead they all drowned. Only three sailors got ashore.

Sydney's worst shipping disaster happened on a dark and stormy night in 1857.

The sailing ship *Dunbar* was trying to get into the harbour, carrying a load of emigrants.

It missed the harbour entrance and sailed straight into the cliffs instead.

Only one person survived. For the funeral procession, 20,000 people lined the streets of Sydney.

RIDING *TO THE* RESCUE

Some people were lucky. In 1876 a steamship called the *Georgette* sprung a leak off the coast of WA. The sea got rough. The ship began to fill with water and to drift towards the shore.

The passengers were loaded into lifeboats, but one boat was smashed in half. Luckily Sam Isaacs, an Aboriginal stockman, was watching on the cliff top.

Isaacs galloped back to the farm. He and the daughter of the farmer, a 16-year-old named

Grace Bussell, grabbed some ropes and galloped back again.

They rode down the cliff to the beach and into the surf. The two of them helped to rescue 50 people over four hours. For her courage, Grace had a town in WA named after her. Sam was given a bronze medal and 100 acres of land.

SHIPS OF THE DESERT

Some passengers were four-legged. From the 1860s to 1901 the colonies shipped in thousands of camels. Expert camel handlers were needed too, so more than 2000 men travelled with them from the places we now call the Middle East, Afghanistan, Pakistan, India, Turkey and Egypt. Europeans down-under called them all 'Afghans'.

In the 1890s, cameleer Abdul Wade challenged a European to a race – from Bourke to Wanaaring and back – 360 kilometres all up. Wade rode a camel and the other rider a horse. The horse got to Wanaaring first, but it died of exhaustion before it could ride back to Bourke.

Camels were better than horses and wagons for taking people and their gear through inland Australia. They can go a long way without food and water, and can carry up to 300 kilograms each. They were called the 'ships of the desert'.

Cameleers assisted explorers, carried goods to the coast and took supplies to outback settlers and the men who built the telegraph line across Australia. The railway that runs from Adelaide to Darwin is named 'the Ghan' in their honour.

They were not the first Muslim people down-under (remember the Macassans?) but they did build Australia's first mosque in 1861, out in SA's outback. The building is no longer there, but a million wild camels are still wandering around the desert.

BLACKBIRDING

Tough as the sea journey to Australia was, at least emigrants chose to come. Colonists wanted cheap labour after Britain stopped sending out convicts in 1843. They found underhanded ways to get workers.

Between 1863 and 1901, 60,000 Pacific Islanders were shipped to Queensland to work in the sugar and cotton fields. They had no choice, like the convicts, but they hadn't committed a crime. Some were tricked into coming. Many were kidnapped.

Traders referred to this as 'blackbirding', as if the islanders were birds to be caught.

> The English vessels pursued their frail canoes, ran them down, and sank them ... Then, while struggling in the sea, the men were seized and thrust into the hold, and the hatches were fastened down. When the ship was filled with a steaming mass of human beings, the captains set sail for Queensland.

Alexander Sutherland, an 1890s historian

The islanders were sold in Queensland for about £9 each (about the cost of a horse). They were fed bad rations and paid only once a year – a fifth of normal wages. The government did very little to stop this trade. If the men tried to escape, they were arrested. They didn't have a hope, since one of the men running the 'blackbirding' business in the 1860s was actually the Premier of Queensland.

OUTBACK TO FRONT

Life in the bush was not what European settlers expected. They didn't have megafauna to deal with any more, but they still had snakes, spiders, floods and flies, and an unpredictable climate.

In the 1800s, Henry Browne Hayes had a problem with snakes in his Sydney mansion, Vaucluse House. They were even sliding into his bed.

He came from Ireland, where there are no snakes – snakes are supposed to hate Irish bog. So Hayes had 500 barrels of bog shipped out from Ireland. He put it in trenches around the house. 'Strange to say,' said a colonist in the 1830s, 'from that time forward Sir Henry Hayes was not visited by snakes . . .'

But he might have been visited by wild goats or pigs. They were dangerous too. Even in towns.

> ... a child was dreadfully mangled by a ferocious sow in Little Flinders Street, and more recently a child has had its ear torn off by a pig at New Town.

Port Phillip newspaper, 1841

WHERE IS THE WATER?

In the strange land down-under, one season the country was as green as England. The next, whole rivers disappeared. There were severe droughts in 1791–1793, the early 1840s, the 1860s, 1880s and 1890s. Sounds as though there were as many droughts as good years, doesn't it?

> No-one who has not lived
> through a drought can
> realise the horrors of it ...
> gaunt, phantom-looking sheep
> dragging their bones into
> the waterhole ... there perhaps
> to bog and be too weak to get
> out.

Katie Langloh Parker, northern NSW, 1890s

BARCOO *ROT*

Convicts were often sent way out in the country to look after herds of sheep. Some men went mad with loneliness. Others got a disease called 'barcoo rot'. Scratches wouldn't heal and blisters appeared on the backs of their hands. If the rot got worse, the shepherd's gums got sore and his teeth fell out.

When money was short so was the menu. Settlers in the bush ate mutton, bread and tea for breakfast, lunch and dinner, all through the week. The bush diet wasn't just boring, it was also dangerous.

'Barcoo rot' was another name for scurvy. Scurvy is a lack of Vitamin C from not eating fresh fruit and vegetables. It killed sailors on long sea voyages too.

Mutton: sheep meat.

Not all meals were mutton, however. Eels also made the menu when Governor Macquarie had guests. Or perhaps you would prefer a dish of kangaroo brains from Australia's first cookbook? Delicious!

Recipe for Slippery Bob
Take kangaroos brains and mix with flour and water, and make into batter; well season with pepper, salt etc; then pour a table-spoonful at a time into an iron pot containing emu fat and take them out when well done. 'Bush fare' requiring a good appetite and excellent digestion.

Edward Abbott,
The English and Australian Cookery Book, 1864

WOULD YOU LIKE SUGAR WITH THAT?

Shops in the bush often weren't much more than 'a piece of canvas stretched over a pole'. One 'store' in 1839 near the Murray River sold only one item: brown sugar.

GIVE IT A BASH

Despite the hardships, people got together
and made their own fun in the bush. The first
Australians invented the original Aussie Rules –
a game called 'marngrook' was played by the
Gunditjmara people in Victoria with a possum-skin
ball. In the photo above, some Queensland gents
had a game of table tennis going with gold-mining
tools, in about 1890.

HOME SWEET *HOME*

Homes, like the one in the photo on the left, were not much fancier than the shops. A settler in 1852 joked that her hut was 'very airy'. It was built from slabs of wood, with a bark roof, and the wind blew through the cracks. It would have been pretty hard to keep your room tidy back then, wouldn't it?

A bathroom was a 'luxury' that 'folks can do without,' she wrote. She probably had a pit dunny, at a distance from the house. But what about toilet paper? The sheep came in handy again. Fleece is quite soft on bottoms.

Settlers tried all sorts of things to stay nice and clean down-under. But it wasn't long before they discovered that the dirt itself contained hidden treasure ...

ALL THAT GLITTERS IS GOLD

The land down-under was keeping a secret. Billions of years back, a rare and beautiful metal was forged beneath the earth's surface. It had been spat out by volcanoes, then washed down into rock cracks and rivers. The first Australians didn't have much use for it. But the new Australians did. They prized gold very, very highly.

When a man named William Clarke found some in the Blue Mountains of NSW he took it to Governor Gipps. The Governor was alarmed. What would happen if the convicts found out? 'Put it away, Mr Clarke,' he said, 'or we shall all have our throats cut!'

So Clarke put it away. At least until Gipps
left the colony. The treasure down-under stayed
a secret. But not for long.

GOLDEN *SOIL*

Seven years after Clarke's find, gold was discovered
in California. People rushed to America from all
over the world, including Australia.

The new Governor began to worry that the colony
was losing too many people. He offered a reward for
finding gold in Australia.

In 1851, a man called Edward Hargraves stepped
forward. He told everybody he had found a rich
goldfield near Bathurst in NSW. His story was
later shown to be as murky as mud. He had taken
someone else's gold. But that didn't matter. There
was gold to be found and the news was out. It took
the history of Down Under in a new direction.

W EALTH *FOR* TOIL

Sydney went gold-crazy overnight. The pavements
were cluttered with 'picks, pans and pots and the
gold-washing machine'. Shops shut, and schools
closed. Shepherds and servants left their jobs to

seek their fortunes. One English woman complained that Sydney ladies still at home had to 'open the door themselves. No servants are to be had, and many of the best and pleasantest families are driven out of the country by it'. Poor things!

Gold was found in Victoria too, a couple of months later. The rush was on. Thousands of people set to work like a plague of rabbits, digging holes across the country.

The bush was cut down and rivers were re-routed. Enormous amounts of gold were found. Between 1851 and 1861, one third of the world's gold came from Victoria.

The discovery of gold affected everyone in unexpected ways.

1. **How many ships were stranded at Port Phillip, Victoria in 1852 because the sailors had run off to the diggings?**

A) 1   B) 2
C) 10   D) 50

Gold! Here I come.

2. **How many people came to Australia during the gold rush?**

A) 5000 per week at the peak time

B) Four times the number of convicts that were sent to Australia

C Double the Australian population
   before the rush
D More than 700,000 people

3. **In 1853, Britain stopped sending
   convicts to Tasmania because:**
A everyone was rich and there
   was no more crime
B there were no ships left to send them in
C the government did not want people
   to commit crimes just to get a free trip
   to Australia
D there was nobody left in Tasmania

DIRTY **WORK**

Gold-digging was dirty and dangerous. River gold
ran out quickly. After that, hopeful gold hunters had
to dig deep shafts on the land they claimed. Diggers
often died when a shaft collapsed or flooded with
water. Others fell down the holes in the dark of
night or were hit by buckets that fell in.

The thousands of miners did not have houses.
Or fridges. Butcher shops were so thick with flies
that 'the air is black and the sound is like thunder',
said a miner. There weren't any toilets either. More
than gold flowed in the river water.

Shafts: holes dug down into the ground to find seams of gold.

The idea of walking up to the goldfield in a couple of days, and shovelling up a few sack-bags full of gold, and going home again, is very charming, and quite as true as Aladdin's lamp.

William Howitt, English history author, 1852

LUCKY *HORSESHOES*

Some people made a lot of money without lifting a spade. In 1855, the first election in Beechworth, Victoria, was held. A shop owner called Daniel Cameron wanted to become a politician. On election day he hired a horse from a circus. Castor the horse was trained to lie on his back and wave his feet in the air. He had been shod with golden horseshoes.

When Castor led a procession into town, his gold

shoes became famous far and wide. Beechworth had so much gold, people said, 'even the miners' horses were shod with it'.

More diggers rushed to Beechworth. More diggers meant more sales for Cameron's shop. He got rich, even if the diggers didn't. The circus kept the horseshoes, which were possibly painted iron, not gold.

He, he, he!

Mr Cameron strikes "gold" with Castor, the circus horse.

SHIFTY *BUSINESS*

The diggings could also be violent and lawless. Miners slept with a loaded gun beside them. At twilight the air was filled with gunfire as diggers shot their firearms into the air before re-loading for the night.

The Victorian Governor said that the goldfields were 'honeycombed with hundreds or thousands of ready-made graves'.

Riches were sometimes got by shifty methods, not by shifting soil.

Dirty tricks included:

- 'Jumping' a claim – taking over someone else's patch of dirt.
- Making up stories about a new rush somewhere else, to get other diggers to move away.
- Pinching other people's equipment.
- Taking gold from your mate's pan.
- Murdering other diggers.

LICENCE *TO* DRILL

The Victorian government also saw a way to make money without digging. Since the land belonged to 'the Crown', they charged diggers a licence fee.

Governor Charles Hotham told diggers they must pay for 'liberty and order', which sounded fair enough. When he visited the goldfields, he was treated like a celebrity. Cheering crowds of 25,000 people turned up to greet him with flags and marching bands. They even took the horses off his carriage and pulled it into town themselves.

But the Governor allowed police to keep part of the licence fee, and so the police put more energy into chasing fees than chasing thieves and bushrangers.

They arrested diggers who had a licence but weren't carrying it. New diggers were often fined the moment they arrived, before they had a chance to buy one. Diggers got more and more unhappy about the licence system.

THE BATTLE OF BALLARAT

In 1853, 5000 people signed a petition in protest. They said they were 'loyal and devoted' to Queen Victoria and had 'a love of law and order'. They just wanted fees and fines reduced.

In October the next year, a digger was bashed to death in Ballarat by the owner of the Eureka Hotel. Many diggers had been murdered before. What really angered people this time was that the authorities didn't punish the hotel owner.

A crowd of diggers rioted and set fire to the hotel. Police helped the owner escape and arrested some of the diggers. The Governor sent extra troops to Ballarat, while diggers held big protest meetings.

```
We swear by the Southern Cross
to stand truly by each other,
and defend our rights and
liberties.
```

Diggers' oath, sworn at Ballarat,
30 November 1854

The police chief didn't like the diggers' attitude. 'We will stand no more of this nonsense,' he said. He ordered another licence hunt on 30 November. An angry crowd of miners gathered in response.

Over the next two days, diggers built a stockade on the Eureka field and raised the blue-and-white Southern Cross flag.

To the government, it looked like a rebellion in the making. But of the thousands of men who went to meetings, only 1500 helped to build the stockade and only 150 stayed to defend it. Most of them went back to their tents to sleep, thinking that the troops wouldn't attack overnight.

But they did – before dawn on the morning of 4 December. It was a short and brutal fight – 22 diggers were killed and six troopers. About 120 diggers were arrested.

238

The other miners did not take up arms as the government had feared. It looked like the Eureka rebels had failed.

But people across Victoria were shocked and sympathetic to the diggers. When the rebels were tried for treason, the jury declared the first 10 'not guilty'. So Hotham gave up. He set the arrested diggers free. He also got rid of the monthly licence fee and gave diggers the right to vote in the new Victorian parliament in 1855.

ALL DIGGERS ARE EQUAL

The gold rush turned the Australian countryside and its society upside down, and stirred all sorts of people into one big mix.

> The equality system here would stun even a Yankee.
> We have all grades and classes.
> We are all mates.

John Capper, *The Emigrant's Guide to Australia*, 1853

Ex-convicts worked next to gentlemen; English next to their enemies the French, Irish and Russians. People came from everywhere to dig for gold – from China, America and all over Europe.

Treason: betraying your ruler or your country.

BUT SOME ARE MORE EQUAL THAN OTHERS

Not everyone was included in the miners' ideas about rights and liberty. Aboriginal people weren't. The mining boom meant that their riches – their homes, sacred places, fresh water and food sources – were dug up or ruined. You can imagine what they must have thought of that.

Chinese diggers weren't offered rights and liberty either. In the month before the Eureka Stockade, a Melbourne newspaper worried about the Chinese miners causing 'serious evils' because of 'the peculiarities of their language, dress and habits of life'. The writer meant that they were different and therefore suspicious.

In 1855 the Victorian government saw another opportunity to make some cash. They began to charge a £10 tax on every Chinese person who landed. There were no protest meetings, petitions or stockades by other diggers over this tax.

It didn't stop the Chinese men coming. Ship captains got round the problem. They sailed past Melbourne instead and stopped on the South Australian coast. The passengers then walked 300–400 kilometres back to the goldfields.

By 1861 there were 38,000 Chinese men living

in Australia (but only 11 Chinese women). There were strong Chinese communities in Melbourne and Bendigo – Australia's first Chinese temples were built there in 1856.

Prospectors also moved north to goldfields in NSW and Queensland. But the other miners did not make them welcome. At the goldfield Lambing Flat in central NSW, there were several violent riots. In 1861, a mob of 2000 European diggers armed themselves with pick handles and whips – that's more than the number of diggers who built the Eureka Stockade.

They attacked the Chinese camp, burnt down tents and beat up Chinese diggers. Nobody is known to have been killed, although there were horrible injuries. Troops and police did arrive to restore order. But the NSW government also brought in a law to stop more Chinese people from coming.

By then gold was running low. Some of the Chinese diggers went home. The men who stayed started businesses or found other work, like growing vegetables and making furniture.

Oh, lucky me
A nugget
of Gold!

AUSTRALIA'S FIRST SCHOOL

AUSTRALIAN FIRSTS

New riches paid for new projects. In this list you can see how much happened in one century. And how Australia was turning into the place we know today.

- **1793** The first school opened down-under.
- **1803** Australia's first newspaper, the *Sydney Gazette*, was published. It was printed and controlled by the government.
- **1814** Governor Macquarie created the colony's first money of its own, by punching a hole in Spanish dollar coins.
- **1817** Australia's first bank, called the Bank of New South Wales, opened its doors.
- **1835** Australia's first political party, the Australian Patriotic Association, was started.

- **1841** The first Australian children's book, *A Mother's Offering to Her Children*, was published in Sydney. It did not become a classic.

- **1852** Australia's first university was started in Sydney.

- **1853** The first steamship to carry mail from England arrived in Australia. People in the colony finally got news from Europe that was less than two months old.

- **1854** The first four kilometres of Australian railway was built between Port Melbourne and Flinders Street in Melbourne. The same line is still used, but by trams, not trains.

- **1854** Geelong man James Harrison invented the world's first 'ice-making machine', or fridge – a very cool claim to fame.

- **1854** Australia's first telegraph line sent messages between Melbourne and Williamstown. By 1877, Melbourne, Adelaide, Sydney, Hobart, Darwin and Perth were all linked by telegraph. The telegraph cable to Hobart ran underwater.

- **1857** Sydney got a sewage system, which

drained raw sewage into the harbour.

- **1859** Australia's first stock exchange began trading in Melbourne, funding new businesses.

- **1868** The first Aussie sports team to tour internationally was an Aboriginal cricket team who went to England. They won or drew 33 out of the 47 matches they played.

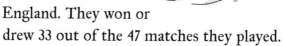

Mum the beach is fun, there's even chocolate in the water!!

- **1872** The first international telegraph message arrived in Adelaide from London. The colonies got messages in hours instead of months.

- **1879** Australia's first National Park was created, south of Sydney. European Australians began to see the natural environment as healthy, not just dangerous or strange. Although they still wanted to 'improve' the bush by planting thousands of foreign trees in the park.

- **1879** The first night footy match was played at the MCG, under the exciting, new wonder of electric lights. It would be a few years (1886) before there was any electric lighting in the streets, though.

NOT SO PROUD *MOMENTS*

Some of Australia's firsts didn't pan out exactly as hoped.

In 1867, Prince Alfred, the son of Queen Victoria, was the first royal visitor to Australia from England. Everyone was very excited but the visit was nearly disastrous. Melburnians rioted over free food and drink at a public banquet. Two boys in Bendigo were burnt to death when a firework display went off early. And the Prince himself was shot and injured in an assassination attempt – another Australian first!

In 1896, Edwin Flack became the first Australian to compete in the Olympics – the only Australian entrant that year. Flack won gold in the 800- and 1500-metre runs. He played a bit of tennis. So far, so good. He'd never run a marathon before (42 kilometres), but he thought he'd give it a red-hot go. Unfortunately, he collapsed after 38 kilometres.

EDWIN FLACK

Australia's swimming hopefuls weren't helped by an 1833 ban on daylight swimming. An Inspector of Nuisances nabbed anyone who went for a dip on a Sydney beach until the end of the century.

WHO'S IN CHARGE?

The early governors of New South Wales held life and death in their hands. There's a list of who they were on pages 138–139. They made all decisions, big and small, about everyone. But that changed as the colonies grew.

In 1823 there was a change in how rules were made down-under. For the first time, a council of five to seven NSW men was appointed by King George IV. Their job was to advise Governor Thomas Brisbane. They could help the Governor to make laws, but the government in Britain could change the laws if it wanted.

The council passed Australia's first legal Act in 1824. You might be wondering, what was so important that it was the reason for our very first Act? Making money is the answer. The Act allowed IOUs to be paid in Spanish dollars, 'to promote trade and just dealing'.

POWER *TO THE* PEOPLE

Gradually, Britain spread the power to make decisions to more people in Australia.

Van Diemen's Land, WA, SA and Victoria got

Act: a written law that lawmakers have voted 'yes', to.

councils too, in 1825, 1832, 1838 and 1851. These councils were gradually made bigger and more powerful. Britain also let some colonists pick some of their own representatives, by voting.

For a while the colony of South Australia was one of the most democratic places in the world. All men over the age of 21 were allowed to vote after 1856, even Aboriginal people. In most states men had to own land to vote, and that did not include traditional landowners.

In 1863 the Victorian government gave 'all ratepayers' the right to vote. They had obviously forgotten that some women were 'ratepayers' too. The newspapers thought it was hilarious when a group of women turned up at an election to give voting a try.

The 'mistake' was soon 'fixed'.

247

AUSTRALIAN LASTS

There were some memorable lasts too. Some were about time. Some were just sad.

- **1840** The last 269 convicts were sent to NSW on the *Eden*. One had escaped from NSW twice, and was being sent back for the third time.
- **1868** The last convict ship, the *Hougoumont*, arrived in WA. It brought the total number of convicts sent here to around 164,000, or over 800 shiploads.
- **1876** Truganini – believed at the time to be the last Tasmanian of only Aboriginal ancestry – died aged 64. Against her wishes, her skeleton was put on display in a museum. She had survived Flinders Island and returned to Tasmania in 1847.
- **1877** The last 62 elderly convicts were removed from Port Arthur in Tasmania and the prison was closed.

Thanks for the sea voyage, but I'd like to go home now!

CORNSTALKS

What were the colonial kids up to, while the adults were exploring, digging and politicking? Growing so tall and healthy compared to British kids that they were called 'cornstalks'.

Colonial families were usually big, so children often had lots of brothers and sisters to play with. They didn't have many bought toys, but they made ragdolls and cubbies. They played games like cricket, hide-and-seek and early versions of footy.

Bush kids liked to hunt possums and quolls and collect insects. City kids had fun knocking on doors and asking to see imaginary people with made-up names, the crazier the better.

Kids also played 'blind man's buff'. In this game a person in a blindfold has to chase others by sound – a good way to knock yourself out in a paddock full of trees!

But it wasn't all fun and games. Children were treated like mini-adults in lots of ways.

```
The Australian boy is a slim,
dark-eyed, olive-complexioned
young rascal ... He is fond
of Cavendish, cricket and
chuckpenny, and systematically
insolent [rude] to all servant
girls, policemen and new-
chums. He is out in the world
at ten years of age, earning
good wages.
```

Frank Fowler, English visitor to Australia in 1859

'Cavendish' was a type of sweet tobacco. It sounds strange, but back then the colonies had no laws to stop children from smoking, drinking alcohol or working.

I just love anarchy!

I felt fine until the doctor came.

flies

Hello, Mr. Runaway Leech.

KILL OR CURE?

Colonial medicine could be as bad as the disease. Next time you're crook, would you like to try leeches, electric shocks or pills that make you vomit? If you had the runs, would you eat chalk mixed with the dangerous drug opium, as an 1853 book suggested? Or how about the poison cyanide dissolved in water to cure hiccups?

Tobacco also had medical uses. The pump kit in the picture was used to wake unconscious people. Not by putting air into their lungs – by blowing smoke up their backside.

GET TO WORK

Almost all children worked, either helping on the farm or in a job.

It might sound great to make your own money, but you didn't get to spend it. If a parent got sick or lost their job, families survived on the wages of their children, which were less than adults' wages.

All the jobs below were done by children. Which one would you like?

- Stockman – rounds up cattle
- Washerwoman – washes other people's clothes
- Bullocky's assistant – helps load stuff on a dray and manage a team of bullocks
- Apprentice carriage maker
- Board boy or rouseabout – clears sheep fleeces from the shearing board
- Scullery maid – washes dishes and helps the cook
- Seamstress – sews clothes
- Shoe-shine boy
- Housemaid – carries hot water and firewood, cleans the house

Bullocks: bulls, but minus their 'bits', used to pull a dray or a cart.

- Stable hand – cleans stables and looks after the horses' gear
- Gardener
- Errand boy or girl for a shopkeeper
- Match seller
- Blacksmith apprentice – makes horseshoes and iron tools

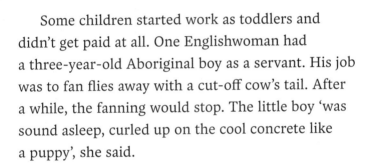

Some children started work as toddlers and didn't get paid at all. One Englishwoman had a three-year-old Aboriginal boy as a servant. His job was to fan flies away with a cut-off cow's tail. After a while, the fanning would stop. The little boy 'was sound asleep, curled up on the cool concrete like a puppy', she said.

'THE GRINDING PROCESS'

Australia had no primary school system for 60 years after the First Fleet. Teachers and churches ran private lessons, but parents had to pay for those. Plenty of them didn't pay and their kids never went.

It wasn't until the 1880s that the law said children had to go to school. Even then, almost all children finished school around the age of 12.

> A taste for reading is a source of happiness and cheerfulness through life, and a shield against its ills.

The Fourth Reading Book for the Use of Schools in Australia, Tasmania and New Zealand, 1876

A single teacher might teach up to 100 kids. Teachers could do what they liked in the classroom. A girl in the 1870s had a teacher who kept a riding whip beside her. 'As often as not lessons were punctuated by short sharp cracks. If these failed, she got up and went for the student with the whip.' Sounds fun, doesn't it?

Lessons were learned by 'the grinding process': the whole school stood up together, in rows facing the board. The teacher read lines off the board, pointing to the words or numbers with a stick. All the students repeated after the teacher. Imagine doing that from seven in the morning until nine at night, which were the hours of one church school in 1832. At that school, the boys learned Latin 'morning, noon and night'.

For a change you might practise handwriting. Students copied sentences on learning to be a better person. Their books were all about Britain and hardly thought Australia worth mentioning. When they did, they weren't very nice about it.

```
The geography [book] said: 'The
inhabitants of New Holland are
amongst the lowest and most
degraded to be found on the
surface of the earth.'
```

Henry Lawson, writing
about school in the 1870s

By the 1880s, schooling was supposed to be available to every child who was 'clean, clad and courteous' as the NSW Education Minister ordered.

But that wasn't always true …

'CLEAN, CLAD AND COURTEOUS'

In 1891 some parents of students in central NSW complained: 'The children from the blacks' camp are coming to this school. In consequence of their filthy habits and appearance they are unfit to be among white children.'

A government inspector visited. He said he 'never saw anything untidy about the black children, or dirty'. He recommended that 'this petition be refused'. The teacher backed him up. But the non-Aboriginal parents wouldn't let their kids go to class and stopped paying their school fees.

The government gave in and started a different school for Aboriginal families. It wasn't the last separate school for Aboriginal children. Nor was it the first – that was the Parramatta Native Institution started by Governor Macquarie in 1815. If you went to that school, you weren't allowed to leave.

But Aboriginal people weren't the only ones getting a rough deal. In this society run by men, half the population was at a serious disadvantage.

THE (UN)FAIRER SEX

You might have noticed that a lot of the stories here are about men. An upside-down fact of life down-under was that Britain had sent a lot more men to the colony than women. Even 50 years after the First Fleet, colonial men still outnumbered women by more than two to one.

Did that mean women were treated well? No. The opposite was true. The early colonies were rough places for girls and women.

```
As for the distresses of
the women, they are past
description.
```

Letter from a female convict, 1788

FEMALE *FACTORIES*

Convict women and their children were separated from the men and sent to 'Female Factories' – prisons in NSW and Van Diemen's Land. This was supposed to be for their protection. But the conditions were bad and the death rate was high.

The NSW Factory was supposed to house about 60 women and children. But in 1817 there were around 200 living and working there.

In the 1830s, riots broke out. Soldiers were sent to frighten the women into good behaviour. Instead the female convicts threw furniture, plates and stones at the soldiers. Eventually the soldiers imprisoned the leaders and the Factory quietened down.

To lower the numbers, Factory women were married off. They were lined up for men to choose, like 'so many cattle' in a market, one man said in 1837. 'The convict goes up and looks at the women and if he sees a lady that takes his fancy he makes a motion to her and she steps to one side. Then they have some conversation together.'

If the lady was 'agreeable', then she left the Factory as the man's wife. If she didn't like him afterwards, that was too bad. Women could also be picked by employers in the same random way. And life wasn't much better once they got out to the bush.

It was a common occurrence for stockmen to exchange their wives with one another, or sell them for a pound of tobacco or a keg of rum.

Mrs McMaugh, country NSW, 1860s.

The law didn't give women much protection.

1. **Guess the age at which girls could marry:**
   Ⓐ 12
   Ⓑ 16
   Ⓒ 18
   Ⓓ 21

2. **When she married:**
   Ⓐ All of a girl's property became her husband's to do what he liked with.
   Ⓑ She could not sue or be sued without her husband.
   Ⓒ No divorce was allowed until the 1860s, and after that only the man could ask for one.
   Ⓓ All of the above.

Answers: 1a (under the law in 1843), 2d

Sue: take legal action against someone who has wronged you, often asking for money.

FLIGHT OF FAIR GAME

From the 1830s, the British government encouraged single women to travel down-under as free settlers. They wanted to even up the numbers of men and women in the colony. In this 1832 cartoon, women are butterflies, flying across the sea. On the shore at Hobart, men are waiting for them. One of them has a big butterfly net. 'I spies mine,' shouts another man.

The title 'A flight of Fair Game' has a double meaning. The butterflies are 'fair' because they are pretty – women were called 'the fairer sex'. But they were also 'fair game' for the men to catch and keep.

THE WEAKER SEX

Women were also called the 'weaker sex'. It was fashionable for women to be droopy, soft and quiet.

> Our silliness, our uselessness, our 'calm repose' is the very thing that gentlemen of the nineteenth century seem to admire.

Woman's letter to a newspaper, 1869

People thought studying was too hard for girls and might make them sick. So their education was different to boys'. Girls in 1867 were told 'to keep your hands soft, to avoid all kinds of work and exercise, try and play music if you can, but never mind arithmetic, it is getting vulgar'.

Vulgar: lacking good taste.

A CAGE *OF CLOTHES*

Female clothes made life even trickier. Girls always wore dresses. Underneath, they wore skirts, called petticoats. If you were rich and fashionable, you might wear as many as six petticoats at once. In England, they helped keep you warm. In Australia, they got in the way.

As girls grew up, their dresses got longer and fancier. To hold their skirts out, women wore big hoops underneath. To hold their tummies in, they wore corsets, laced up tightly.

The longer her dress, the less adventurous a girl could be. Running, climbing trees and riding a horse the normal way was impossible.

One Victorian girl called this 'a tyranny of garments' – clothes ruled over what a woman could do.

But some women thought it was time for change.

Chirp! Chirp! Chirp!

LOUISA LAWSON
1848–1920

Louisa Lawson didn't have an easy life. She wanted
to be a teacher, but her father made her leave school
at 13. Then she married at 18 and lived in a tent. She
was determined to make life better for herself and
others. In 1883, she moved from the country to Sydney
with her four children. As a single mum, she earned
money by sewing and washing. She did a lot more too.

She set up a hostel for young working women. She
started a club, called the Womanhood Suffrage League,
to argue for giving women a vote as men's equals. She
wrote poems and speeches, and published her son
Henry's first book. Henry became one of Australia's
most famous writers.

Lawson's biggest success came in 1888 – she started
Australia's first magazine for women. Lawson wrote
and printed *The Dawn* herself. It had useful tips on
how to get grease out of wallpaper – iron it – and how
to get insects out of your ears – put oil in them! But
The Dawn's main aim was 'to fight women's battles'. It
talked about issues like divorce, education and voting.

Follow man no longer as his
slave. Advance; if he does
not keep pace, be his leader.

Louisa Lawson's advice to women,
The Dawn, July 1892

Lawson was a 'printing ink champion', as *The Dawn* said about itself. Male printers did not like Lawson hiring women and selling her paper. She and her female workers were hassled by unwanted visitors. Lawson poured a bucket of water over one man. Then she threatened him with printing ink. He left before she coloured in his nice white suit.

He wasn't the only one who thought Lawson's actions were too much. But her arguments made a difference and inspired others – South Australian women got the vote in 1894. Other states followed. Despite the obstacles in her way, Louisa Lawson was a strong voice for Australian women.

HALF A MAN

Many women in the Colony needed to work, despite their cumbersome clothes and patchy education. Back in 1841, Caroline Chisholm saw that 'when pretty girls have no money and no friends, Sydney is a very bad place for them'. So she started Australia's first job agency for women. But there were no laws to say how they should be paid. Women were paid about half what men were.

They were also kept out of many jobs. Universities down-under wouldn't let women study at first, and then only some subjects. They weren't allowed to do medicine, for example.

The lives of the 'fairer sex' were clearly anything but fair. Yet the 'weaker sex' was anything but weak. By the end of the 1800s, lots of women (and some men) tried to do something about it.

One young woman called Clarence Stone went to America and England to study. She came back in 1890 as Australia's first female doctor. A few years later she and 10 others started a hospital 'for women, by women'.

Women formed groups to push for better treatment. They argued for changes to laws about property, marriage and alcohol. And they didn't stop there. They wanted to be part of law-making.

ROLL UP, ROLL *UP!*

When they weren't dealing with earwigs and irons, women wanted a say in choosing the government. Men objected.

If a woman got the vote, some said, 'she would lose her gentle and affectionate disposition'. Men worried that women would stop being nice and politics might distract them from their 'proper duties' as housewives. They might start getting crazy ideas about going into parliament, getting paid a proper wage or joining the army.

In 1891, the Premier of Victoria, James Munro, said he would bring in a law allowing women to vote, if enough women wanted it.

Victorian women organised a petition asking for what was called suffrage.

```
Your petitioners believe: That
Government of the People by
the People and for the People
should mean all the People, and
not one half ... That in short,
Women should Vote on equal
terms with men.
```

The Women's Suffrage Petition, 1891

Suffrage: the right to vote.

The Premier's wife was the second person to sign the petition. In just a few weeks, so many women signed that the petition reached 260 metres (over five swimming pools) long. It looked like a monster roll of toilet paper. And the politicians treated it like one.

The politicians in parliament were all men, of course. So the change to the law did not pass.

Those hopeful Victorian women who signed the petition wouldn't get to vote until 1906.

THE BOSSES VS THE BOYS

After the convict era, old English ways of running things were being turned on their heads.

'Society is in a topsy-turvy condition,' an English visitor to Adelaide wrote in 1878. She was bothered because 'the men who are at the top of the tree are mainly those who come from nothing'. Other men 'from good families' had low-level jobs.

New ideas about fairness had spread to Australia from Britain. Lots of work and not enough workers also meant that workers here had more clout with their bosses than back in Europe.

888

In 1856, stonemasons in Melbourne exercised their political muscle. They put down their tools and walked off the job. Employers were forced to give the stonemasons and other builders the right to work only eight hours per day.

Melbourne still has old buildings with the symbol '888' carved into the stones. It's not a date – it was more like a team motto.

```
Eight hours to work,
Eight hours to play,
Eight hours to sleep,
Eight bob a day.
A fair day's work,
For a fair day's pay.
```

Nineteenth-century slogan

Bob: a shilling, or 12 pence; enough for a kilogram of apples or two loaves of bread.

But even after 1856, workers still had it tough. They had no sick pay, no minimum wage, no holidays and only Sundays off.

NO FAIR DAY'S PAY

Unfortunately 888 didn't apply to all workers. When gas lighting was installed in the cities, shop workers had to work as long as 14 hours a day. Tradies thought shop workers were 'smooth-faced, snub-nosed rogues', plus they wanted the shops open long hours so they could go shopping after work.

In the bush, farmers often used Aboriginal workers. They knew where to find water and grass, and how to track lost animals. 'I don't know what we pioneers should have done without the blacks,' said a Queensland station owner, 'for they can't be beat at looking after horses and cattle'.

What she doesn't mention is that they were also cheap. 'A white man costs £52 per year and his food,' said a West Australian farmer in 1882. 'A native will do the same work for his food, and a shirt occasionally.' Aboriginal workers were whipped or beaten if they didn't do what the boss wanted. It was often the only way for them to stay on their land.

In WA, Aboriginal men and women did the athletic, dangerous work of 'skin-diving' for pearls

Minimum wage: the smallest amount of money a boss can legally pay a worker.
Skin-diving: diving deep underwater with bare skin, holding a heavy stone (and your breath), many divers died.

and oyster shells. Malay, Japanese, Filipino and Torres Strait Islander people were later brought in to dive alongside them. 888 didn't cover workers from China either, like the men who worked in a northern Australian goldmine in the 1870s and 1880s – another very risky job – and built a railway to Darwin.

Despite this, some non-Europeans down-under did manage to become wealthy bosses. Abdul Wade – originally from Afghanistan – ran a big transport business. Quong Tart (opposite) was a very successful merchant. And Kitamura Toranosuke turned animal hooves, tendons and leg bones into big profits by boiling them and exporting them to Japan.

WORKING TOGETHER

Many colonial workers didn't welcome the competition. They joined together in unions, to negotiate as a group with their employers. They wanted more wages and more rights. And one of the things they wanted was to keep out non-white workers.

By 1890 Australia had 1400 different unions. About one man in six was in a union – from bootmakers to shearers – more than anywhere else in the world. When a union didn't get the pay raise or work conditions they asked for, they stopped work. To really put the pressure on the bosses, other unions joined in.

QUONG TART *1850–1903*

Quong Tart came to Australia from China with his uncle at the age of nine. He made a fortune on the NSW goldfields. Then he made a second fortune importing tea and silk, and running tearooms. A newspaper said that customers went 'not for their tea, but their nice little Tart'.

Quong Tart is as well-known as the Governor himself, and quite as popular among all classes.

Daily Telegraph newspaper, 18 December 1897

Tart liked to play the bagpipes and recite Scottish poetry. He became a British subject in 1871.

Quong Tart was one of Sydney's richest men, but he spent a lot of time and money helping poor people and the Chinese community. Louisa Lawson and the Womenhood Suffrage League also met in his tearooms.

British subject: a person who belongs to the British Empire, the lands ruled by Britain. For a long time after 1788 all Australians were British subjects.

STRIKE *ONE*

Most bosses did not like the unions. In 1890, when ship officers tried to form a new union, Victorian shipowners did not let their employees join.

In August, the ship officers stopped work. Then coalminers joined the strike so the ships had no fuel. Transport workers joined in so the ships couldn't be loaded. Shearers joined in so there was no wool to load on the ships. About 50,000 men had stopped work. Even workers in New Zealand and Fiji went on strike. Melbourne was in darkness because the gas workers were striking. A quarter of Melbourne's population – 100,000 people – marched through Melbourne's streets in protest.

When the government called up special volunteer troops to control the crowds, an army officer instructed them to shoot the protesters.

```
If you are called upon to
charge the people, you must
do your duty unflinchingly,
even though you know your
own brothers and sisters,
were in the crowd. Fire
low and effectively.
```

Colonel Tom Price, speech to troops, 1890

The Colonel's speech started a furious argument in parliament and the newspapers. Luckily, most people were not as trigger-happy as he was so there was no battle in the streets.

Meanwhile the strikers weren't being paid. Other unions donated one day's pay a week from their members. But it wasn't enough.

The bosses found non-union men without jobs to work for them instead. After a couple of months, the workers gave up. When they got back to work, ship officers found that their pay had been cut by up to a third. The bosses definitely won that round.

STRIKE *TWO*

The next year, a sheep-station owner in Queensland gave his shearers a new contract to sign. The contract paid shearers lower wages. It also gave the owner the choice of hiring workers from outside the union if he wanted to. The shearers thought this was a woolly idea.

Contract: an agreement between two people or a business and its workers.

They refused to sign. Shearers across Queensland prepared for a fight. Literally. They held a big protest, carrying the Southern Cross flag. They burnt down woolsheds, found weapons and set up camps outside towns. The Queensland government sent in police and soldiers to protect non-union workers and station owners.

But like the ship officers, it was not violence that ended the strike. It was hunger. The shearers held out for four months, but by then they were starving. They were forced to go back to work.

NO STRIKE THREE

Going on strike hadn't helped the workers much. So some of the leaders formed political parties instead. They aimed to get members elected into parliament and improve things that way.

```
You people of Queensland, who
know the evils existing in
the old country [Britain] -
will you not for the sake of
your wives and little ones
record your votes against the
rack renting slave-owning
landlords?
```

Queensland Labour Party, 1893

In NSW, they called themselves the 'Labour League' and in Queensland the 'Labour Party'. That probably sounds familiar, although today's Labor Party is nicer to the bosses than it was then.

The word 'slave' in the quote sounds extreme. But some landowners did use unpaid Islander and Aboriginal workers – not that the Labour League or Labour Party were interested in sticking up for them. Aboriginal farm workers would have to wait until the 1960s for equal pay.

HOME RUN

The people of Queensland listened to the new Party.

In 1899, the Queensland Labour Party formed a government in Brisbane – the first Labour government in the world. The government only lasted a week, which was not long enough to make big changes. But the Labour Party had shown that politics was for ordinary people too, not just the rich.

And just around the corner was a really big change for the whole country ...

Change !!?

THE STORY CONTINUES ...

Around 400 years ago
Macassans start visiting the north coast of the land down-under to trade

1606
The Dutch ship *Duyfken* lands on Cape York – the first recorded meeting between Aboriginal and European people occurs

1770
Captain Cook explores the east coast of 'New Holland'

1788
Britain sends convicts to Botany Bay, 'New South Wales', on the First Fleet

1789
Smallpox spreads into Aboriginal communities

1790
The Second Fleet of convicts arrives

1803
The first convicts are sent to a settlement in 'Van Diemen's Land'

1808
The military takes over New South Wales in the Rum Rebellion

1813
Blaxland and co. make it over the Blue Mountains

Squatters begin to move onto land all over New South Wales

1824

Britain officially agrees to call the continent 'Australia'

The first convicts are sent to Moreton Bay in Queensland

1814

Australia's first currency is created

1829

Britain claims possession of the whole continent

A colony is started at Swan River, WA, by free colonists

1830

The Black Line tries to force all Aboriginal people out of Tasmania

1836

A colony is started in South Australia by free colonists

1851

The gold rushes begin

1850

Britain separates Victoria from NSW, and SA and Van Diemen's Land are allowed to vote for part of their own governments

1856

An eight hour work day is achieved for some workers

That's a lot happening in only 400 years. But Down Under was still a bunch of colonies owned by Britain. What happened next?

1868

The last convicts arrive in Australia, at Fremantle, WA

1894

SA gives women the vote

THE BABY NATION

Australia's ultimate boss did not live on our continent. All of Australia still belonged to Britain. But people down-under had uppity ideas about that too.

Although the Eureka Stockade was quickly put down, the miners' organisation – the Reform League – had started something even bigger.

```
This League is nothing more
or less than the germ of
Australian independence.
No power on earth can now
restrain the headlong
strides for freedom of
people of this country.
```

Ballarat Times newspaper, 18 November 1854

The newspaper was getting a bit carried away with itself. Most people's 'headlong strides' were towards the goldfields or the squatters' sheep stations, not politics. Australian independence could wait. And it did. But there were baby steps in that direction.

The colony of South Australia gave all its men aged over 21 the right to vote in 1856. It took another 40 years for men across Australia to have that right. On paper that mostly included Aboriginal men, but not in WA and Queensland – right up until the 1960s.

Each colony had its own government, its own taxes, and its own railway system. If a farmer wanted to send his wheat interstate by train, it had to be unloaded from one train and loaded onto another. The farmer also had to pay taxes on those 'foreign' goods. It was very annoying, especially for people who lived near the border of two colonies.

So each colony pretty much did its own thing, in its own time. Soon that got in the way of making money.

A politician in NSW called Henry Parkes suggested to the other colonies that 'the time has arrived when these colonies should be united by some federal bond of connection'. He saw the colonies as 'an infant empire'.

I can achieve federation!

A SLOW BIRTH

That was in 1867. The time had obviously not arrived. The infant took a long time to be born.

By 1881 Parkes had become Premier of NSW. He persuaded the other states to set up a 'Federal Council' to talk about taxes, telegraphs and railways. But then he changed his mind and didn't join.

By 1889, Parkes was getting old. He had been Premier three times. One day, after lunch, he said to the Governor of NSW, 'I could achieve federation of the colonies in twelve months'. He was not very humble about his abilities. 'Why don't you?' the Governor replied. 'It would be a glorious finish to your life.'

A couple of months later Parkes went to talk to the Queensland government about federation. On the way back, he stopped at a town called Tenterfield in NSW and gave a speech. 'I believe that the time has come,' he said. (Again.)

I can achieve Federation! I truly can! I think I can...

It was time to think about 'the creation on this Australian continent of an Australian government and an Australian parliament'.

THE FATHERS OF FEDERATION

The men who set up the nation of Australia were an argumentative lot. Here's what was said about them at the time:

- Henry Parkes, NSW Premier
- Edmund Barton, NSW politician and lawyer
- George Turner, Victorian Premier
- Samuel Griffith, Queensland Premier
- Charles Kingston, SA Premier
- George Reid, NSW Premier
- James Dickson, Queensland Premier
- Alfred Deakin, Victorian politician and lawyer. He secretly wrote anonymous reports for British newspapers and was the author of most of the comments above.

He 'always had in his mind's eye his own portrait as a great man'

A 'fathead'

An 'average man'

'Lean, cold, clear, collected and acidulated'

'A man of great physical size and strength' (who had challenged another politician to a duel)

'Vain and resolutely selfish' with an 'immense, jelly-like stomach'

'Oily Jimmy', a 'prating cockatoo'

Prating Cockatoo, Alfred?

Prating??

Prating? What's that?

I love rubbish!

It means he talks rubbish!

283

PROS AND CONS

Putting all the states together to form a federation
was a grand idea. But there was plenty to argue about.

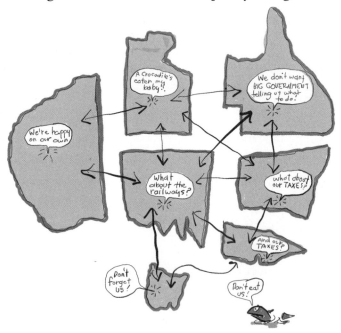

For	**Against**
The continent could have one system for transport and communications.	None of the colonies wanted a federal government telling them what to do.

Federation: a group of states with a central government.

The colonies could get rid of all the different taxes that got in the way of business.

None of the colony governments wanted to lose their taxes.

A single federal government would have more say with Britain and other countries than six squabbling colonies.

Little colonies like Tasmania were afraid they would get no say in the new government.

A federal government could make national laws and keep certain groups of people out (like Islanders, Chinese people and non-white people generally).

Big colonies thought they should get more say in the laws because they had more people.

A federal government could run a single army to protect Australia from possible invasion by countries like Germany, Russia, France or China.

A national army and government would be expensive, and none of the colonies wanted to pay for it.

The colonies were now thinking of themselves as different, and tougher, than people back in Britain. Stories about bush heroes by Banjo Paterson and Henry Lawson helped. So did each cricketing victory against the English. At the same time, however, colonials didn't want to be too different. They wanted Australia to be culturally British and white.

MORE CONS

In 1890 a high-powered bunch of premiers and politicians met for a conference. Out of the conference, in 1891, came a convention (another meeting). Out of the convention finally came something that wasn't a meeting. The colonies agreed to a federal constitution – a set of rules that would tell everyone how the country was to run. But it was only a draft.

It was all pretty *con*fusing for the politicians too.

WHO'S IN? WHO'S OUT?

We could have been Australasia, instead of Australia. Both Fiji and New Zealand were invited to be part of Federation. They both said no.

One New Zealander politician said his colony was much better at giving rights to indigenous

people, thank you very much. New Zealand didn't want to be ruled by a parliament of 'mostly Australians, that cares nothing and knows nothing about native administration'.

He was right that Australian politicians were not very interested in Indigenous citizens. The Constitution ordered that Aboriginal and Torres Strait Islander people were literally not to be counted as members of the population. They had no say in Federation.

And there was more trouble ahead. Not everyone in Australia wanted Federation.

Policians had other things to think about when Victoria's banks went broke in 1891–1893. Lots of people lost money and lost their jobs.

Governments only got interested again when the voters did, starting their own conferences to support Federation.

Eventually, the politicians agreed on the two key points:

Ⓐ How the new federal government would work.

Ⓑ How Australians would vote it in.

YES-NO REID
WRECKS THE VOTE

In June 1898, Tasmania, NSW, Victoria and SA each held a vote on the new constitution. Queensland and WA weren't interested and didn't vote.

Most people in Tasmania, Victoria and SA voted 'yes'. They were furious when NSW Premier Reid campaigned against the constitution. They were stunned when NSW failed to get enough 'yes' votes.

But they didn't give up. Instead the colonies agreed to another round of voting. This time Queensland joined in. The 'yes' vote won across eastern Australia.

WA STEPS UP

But WA was still out. Their politicians weren't interested in joining the federation.

The people in WA's rich goldfields, far away from Perth, weren't happy. They wanted to break off and start a new colony that would become part of Australia. It was going to be called 'Auralia'. The idea of losing all that gold alarmed the WA government and helped them change their mind. WA voted 'yes' in 1900, just a few months before Australia was born.

Auralia: from the Latin word for 'golden', sounds a lot like 'Australia'.

TEA **AND** TOASTS

The land down-under wasn't independent yet. The constitution needed a 'yes' vote from the British government and the Queen.

Representatives from the colonies (except WA) sailed off to London, constitution in hand. When they arrived they were treated very nicely. They even got tea with Queen Victoria.

They went to the races on the royal train. They even went to dinner with the Worshipful Company of Ironmongers – whatever they were. Maybe they were a heavy-metal band.

The representatives asked Britain to pass the constitution without changes.

However, the British politician in charge of the

colonies thought that was pure cheek. He'd 'see them damned first,' he said.

But the colonials didn't back down. In the end, the two sides agreed to change a few of the words, without taking any proposed powers from the Australian government.

Alfred Deakin, Edmund Barton and Charles Kingston – two future Prime Ministers and a Premier – held hands and danced around the room for joy.

One people, one destiny.

Sir Henry Parkes' toast
at a banquet for 900 guests, 1891

On 1 January 1901, Down Under became the nation of Australia.

1 January 1901: a very easy date to remember.

INDEPENDENCE

The fathers of Federation thought independence was a great achievement. And so did a lot of Australians, even though these kids from Melbourne don't look too thrilled.

Parties were held across the country. A Chinese dragon danced on the streets of Melbourne, but as you can see in this photo, most celebrations were very British. These children are dressed in costumes from England, Scotland and Wales. Wearing another country's gear seems an odd way to celebrate your independence – but it shows how close to Britain many Australians still felt.

FEDERATION

Below is a checklist of things you might think every nation needs. Which essentials do you think Australia had at Federation?

- ☐ Name
- ☐ Capital city
- ☐ Flag
- ☐ Currency
- ☐ Government
- ☐ Constitution
- ☐ Head of state
- ☐ National anthem
- ☐ Definition of who is a citizen

In 1901, we only had three of these for our very own – our name, our constitution and a government. We just barely managed the government – Tasmania's representative was only added on New Year's Eve.

Barton was sworn in as the first Prime Minister and Lord Hopetoun – a 'Knight of the

Prime Minister: the head of our federal government – the leader of the political party or team who wins the most votes.

Thistle' – was sent by Queen Victoria to be the first Governor-General.

Even after 1901, we didn't look like modern Australia. For Aboriginal and Torres Strait Islander people and some other Australians, national independence didn't mean personal freedom. As a country we didn't have a capital, a currency, a flag or an anthem. And our citizens were still called 'British subjects'. We had a borrowed currency from England, and Queen Victoria as a shared head of state.

It took us quite a while to organise the rest of the list. And we've still got a British royal as our head of state. Nevertheless, in 1901 we took our place in the world. We became one, separate nation. And unlike many of Britain's colonies around the world, we had managed independence without a war.

In Europe, Asia and America, the spread of civilisation has been behind the broad-sword, the spear, the rifle and the bayonet. The six States of the Australian Commonwealth, however, were cradled in peace.

The Advertiser newspaper, Adelaide, 2 January 1901

Governor-General: The Queen's representative in Australia.

Citizens: people who belong to a certain country with rights and responsibilities.

UPSIDE-DOWN OR RIGHT WAY UP?

Since you've read this far, you have covered 200 million years of history. That's massive. Not many stories are that long.

Now that you know how this ancient land became Australia, you might think the newspaper on the previous page was a tad overexcited about how peaceful our history was. The dinosaurs, the megafauna, and many of the people you've met in these pages might not agree either. But they would probably all tell you that their bit of history matters, however mega or minor it is.

The story of Down Under has an upside and a downside, and a mixed bunch of characters. Maybe people in this book are long-lost relatives of yours. Australia turned out better than some of them expected. All credit to the people who made it so.

Whichever way you look at it, this is our story. And our home. And here we are.

You're about to finish the book, although this isn't the end of Australia's story. After Federation there were even more ups and downs for the land down-under.

For now, though, we have landed the right way up.

Or have we?

ACKNOWLEDGEMENTS

This book has been helped considerably by the
La Trobe University library, the State Library of
Victoria, the National Library, Museum of Queenland,
the Bass and Flinders Centre and the research
of dozens of academic and other historians.

Thank you to the custodians of cultural knowledge who shared their stories and allowed them to
be in this book and others who so generously offered
their time and knowledge, in particular the Murujuga
Circle of Elders and Sean McNeair; Katherine Njamme;
Gugu Badhun elders and Dale Gertz; Magabala Books
and Bill Neidjie's family; Dorothea Randall; Shane
Karpany; Isabel Tarrago; Emily Evans and the family
of Dick Roughsey; Bidjigal elder Laddie Timbery
and grandson Raymond; Andrea Myers and Dillon
Andrews at the Bunuba Dawangarri Aboriginal
Corporation; and Wurundjeri elder Jacqui Wandin.

Special appreciation to Edie Wright for her inval-
uable input and to editor Michelle Madden for her
enormous commitment. Thank you also to Grant Finlay
at Aboriginal Heritage Tasmania for his advice, and to
others who shared their contacts. Every effort was made
to consult and seek permission from relevant people –
apologies for anyone we have overlooked. Please see
alisonlloyd.com.au for a detailed list of sources.